FOR ORGANS, PIANOS & ELECTRONIC KEYBOARDS

E-Z PLAY® TODAY

265

SONGS OF THE 1910's

THE DECADE SERIES

W9-AEX-098

3 1571 00195 2665

ISBN 0-7935-3179-9

HAL•LEONARD
CORPORATION

7777 W. BLUEMOUND RD. P.O. BOX 13819 MILWAUKEE, WI 53213

Ragtime to Wartime

by Patrick Byrne

The dance team of Vernon and Irene Castle as they appeared in the Irving Berlin musical *Watch Your Step* (1914). The Hollywood version of their lives is told in the film *The Story of Vernon and Irene Castle* starring Fred Astaire and Ginger Rogers.

Although the threat of war loomed large in Europe at the beginning of the 1910s, Americans were still enjoying the fruits of the Progressive Age, an exhilarating era in which the United States rose from the ashes of the Civil War to become one of the world's great powers. The potential dangers of a European war seemed very remote on this side of the Atlantic as most Americans still agreed with Washington and Jefferson that the New World should have little to do with the Old.

The dominant musical style during the early years of the decade was an amalgam of ragtime and theater music. Scott Joplin had injected ragtime, a syncopated style of African-American music, into the musical mainstream around the turn of the century with his famous piano rags. However, none of these early rags could match the phenomenal success of Irving Berlin's "Alexander's Ragtime Band" (1911), a pseudo-ragtime song that touched off a fevered craze for "rags" that would last through most of the decade.

The all-out frenzy of these years reflected the dramatic changes that American society was undergoing at this time. Wonderful new inventions were rapidly changing almost every aspect of daily life. Many of the modern conveniences that we take for granted (flying machines, telephones, horseless carriages, motion pictures, sound recordings, etc.) became a reality for most Americans during the 1910s.

A big part of the ragtime mania was the dances that accompanied the music. Before ragtime came on the scene, American social dances generally clung close to their European roots by using polka, waltz, schottishce, or similar rhythms. The popular songs that used these "square" rhythms were quickly swept off the floor by the wild, syncopated ragtime dances popularized by the trend-setting dance team of Vernon and Irene Castle. Both on and off the dance floor, Irene stood American fashion on its ear. Her bobbed hair and trim figure quickly became hallmarks of feminine style for the 1910s and beyond. Vernon, her handsome husband, was an

Ragtime syncopation made social dancing a contact sport in the 1910s. The turkey trot (top) and the grizzly bear (bottom) were just two of the many fad dances that swept across the dance floors of America during this decade.

The cities of America grew rapidly during the 1910s. By 1920, for the first time in the nation's history, a majority of the population lived in urban settings like the one pictured here.

Englishman and a member of the R.A.F. He died in an airplane crash at Fort Worth in 1918 at the age of thirty. Immediately after Vernon's accident, the twenty-five year old Irene retired.

The nation's parents and moral authorities were naturally aghast that the decent dances of their own youth had been replaced almost overnight by a veritable menagerie of immorality: fox trot, fish walk, turkey trot, grizzly bear, bunny hug, kangaroo dip, pigeon wing, lame duck, and camel walk. Add to these provocative dance steps the suggestive gyrations of the notorious ballin' the jack with its frequent bumps and grinds and you can begin to understand why many in the older generation were so upset. Fearing what these sensual dances might unleash, the country's elders were convinced that America's young people were blindly ragging their way to moral ruin.

5

The legendary vaudevillian Sophie Tucker, "The Last of the Red-Hot Mamas," did much to popularize ragtime through her brassy vocal interpretations of songs like "That International Rag."

Although Irving Berlin was not the father of ragtime he was certainly one of its favorite uncles. His 1913 hit "That International Rag" summed up the extent of ragtime's worldwide popularity two years after his "Alexander" had taken the floor.

With their young people ragging up a storm, parents understandably longed for the imagined simplicity of the recent past. Nostalgia has always found expression in popular music in the form of wistful ballads and some of the biggest hits of the 1910s were also some of the decade's most endearing songs: "I Want a Girl (Just Like the Girl that Married Dear Old Dad)" (1911); "Moonlight Bay" (1912); "My Melancholy Baby" (1912); and "Indiana (Back Home Again in Indiana)" (1917). All of these sentimental tunes were delightfully old-fashioned the day they were written and they have represented the nostalgic ideal of several generations of Americans.

In 1903 a journalist coined the term Tin Pan Alley to describe the burgeoning music industry that was located along New York City's 28th Street. The publishers and composers who inhabited Tin Pan Alley became tremendously

Irving Berlin at the time of "Alexander's Ragtime Band." The ragtime hits of this twenty-four year old composer freed him from the poverty of New York City's tenement slums and launched an incredible song-writing career that would last five decades.

successful during the first quarter of the century. Between 1900 and 1910 almost 100 songs had sold over a million copies of sheet music. With sales figures like these becoming more common, a publisher and a composer could, for the first time, realistically hope to earn about $100,000.00 each if one of their songs "hit it big." In 1910 "Let Me Call You Sweetheart" and "Down by the Old Mill Stream" were both published and they each sold over six million copies of sheet music. With these two blockbusters setting the pace, total sheet music sales for that one year alone reached an all-time high of two billion copies. Tin Pan Alley had clearly become big business and in 1913 Billboard magazine printed its first weekly tabulation of music sales, a listing that soon became, and still remains, the accepted measure of success in the music business.

Not far from Tin Pan Alley, the Broadway theater district was also becoming a hotbed of creative and commercial activity as many of the decade's hits were spawned on its stages. Vaudeville was at its zenith during this decade and the most famous vaudeville theater of all, the legendary Palace, opened in New York City in 1913. Among the headliners who worked this stage were names that would dominate

American popular entertainment for decades to come: George Jessel, Will Rogers, Eddie Foy, Nora Bayes, Sophie Tucker, Eddie Cantor, Fanny Brice, The Marx Brothers, Jimmy Durante, Bill Robinson, Mae West, Burns and Allen, and Houdini. Typical of the songs that made vaudeville famous was Bert Williams' "Play that Barber Shop Chord."

Lavish revues — such as Florenz Ziegfeld's series of *Follies*, begun in 1907 — provided theatergoers with a new, more sophisticated alternative to vaude-

Nora Bayes was a *Follies* star of the first magnitude. Married five times, Bayes lively personal life set the standard for generations of film sirens and pop prima donnas to come. Hollywood told the story of her second marriage in the 1944 movie *Shine on Harvest Moon* starring Ann Sheridan.

Bert Williams was one the most popular entertainers of the 1910s. W.C. Fields called this African-American comedian "the funniest man in the world, and the saddest." A long-time headliner in vaudeville, Williams' poignant portrayals of a hapless little man preceded Charlie Chaplin's little tramp by a generation. Williams died at the age of 47 in 1922.

ville. Initially, the main attraction of the *Follies* was, of course, the gorgeous Ziegfeld Girls. In the long run — the last *Follies* closed in 1931 — these shows offered more than just girls, girls, and more girls. Among the many musical numbers to come out of the *Follies* were some of the greatest songs of the decade including "Be My Baby Bumble Bee" (1912) and "Peg o' My Heart" (1913).

A third and even more elaborate form of theatrical entertainment, aptly called the *extravaganza*, also became popular during the 1910s. Al Jolson, the most popular entertainer of the decade and possibly of the entire first half of the century, achieved his initial stardom performing in this type of show. Jolson's Broadway debut came at the Winter Garden on March 20, 1911, in an extravaganza entitled *La Belle Paree*.

In another extravaganza, *The Honeymoon Express* (1913), Jolson introduced his signature song "You Made Me Love You." Yet another great Jolson original from this decade was "Rock-A-Bye Your Baby with a Dixie Melody." He introduced that all-time favorite in the extravaganza *Sinbad* in 1918.

Although vaudeville, revues, and extravaganzas were all extremely popular during the 1910s they were really part of America's theatrical past. A new type of stage show, now universally known as the Broadway Musical, was evolving and would eventually overshadow these other types of entertainments to become a permanent part of American popular entertainment.

As an art form distinct from operetta, American musical comedy first came of age in the intimate Princess Theatre shows of 1917-1918: *Oh, Boy!, Leave It to Jane,* and *Oh, Lady! Lady!!* With music by Jerome Kern and book and lyrics by P.G. Wodehouse and Guy Bolton, these charming, well-integrated scores had believable story lines about Middle Class America. The style established by Kern, Wodehouse, and Bolton would be widely imitated, leading to a veritable explosion of musical comedy on Broadway in the 1920s.

Even if you lived far from New York's Great White Way, live stage performances were still the norm in 1910. All across America every self-respecting city of any size had it's Opera House or Music Hall where touring troops of vaudevillians would perform. But this was a dying tradition as doomed as the horse-drawn carriage. A new technology in the form of inexpensive sound recordings was destined to become the dominant factor in the nation's music and entertainment industry. By the end of the decade almost all of the hit songs were available on phonograph records

as well as sheet music. A few years later, in the Roaring Twenties, the quaint custom of gathering around the parlor piano to sing songs with your family and friends had generally given way to passively listening to music on the Victrola or via radio broadcasts.

Motion pictures were in their infancy during the 1910s. Nickelodeons provided very inexpensive entertainment and they began replacing live shows early in the decade. "Talkies" were still a decade away but the rapidly growing interest in silent movies already had an effect on the music business by the end of the decade. Early film music like "Mickey" (1917) was

At first, the Victrola had to compete with the pianola, or player piano, as the most modern and convenient way to bring music into the parlors of America. Phonograph records won that battle and in the coming decades the familiar black disks eclipsed all other musical formats including sheet music.

The Tramp, Charlie Chaplin's immortal screen persona, was first brought to life in 1914 during a series of thirty-five films that Chaplin made at Mack Sennett's Keystone studio.

The brilliant comedienne Mabel Normand, pictured here at the age of twenty three, was once described by director Mack Sennett as being "as beautiful as a spring morning." Their romantic relationship is the subject of the 1974 Broadway musical *Mack and Mabel*.

written to accompany the silent action taking place on the screen.

In 1910 the population of the United States was quickly approaching one hundred million. The nation had grown by nearly twenty million since the turn of the century and would grow by at least another ten million by the end of the decade. Much of this phenomenal growth came from the seemingly endless wave of immigrants who were desperately fleeing the troubles in Europe. The song "Don't Bite the Hand That's Feeding You" (1915) gives us one view of the tension that this sudden influx of "foreigners" had caused.

By the middle of the decade, Americans could no longer deny the grave situation in Europe. On June 28, 1914, the Austrian Archduke Ferdinand was assassinated by a Serbian in Sarijevo. This was the spark that ignited the European powder keg and began World War I, the so-called "War To End All Wars." The hostilities lasted four years and the War officially ended with the Treaty of Versailles in 1919. The human cost of the War was be staggering. The military casualties alone amounting to ten million dead.

In 1915 the sinking of the passenger ship Lusitania by a German submarine with the loss of 1,198 lives, including 128 U.S. citizens, nudged American public opinion away from neutrality toward the British-French side of the conflict.

The sinking of the New York bound Lusitania off the Irish coast by a German submarine on May 7, 1915, tested America's desire to avoid becoming involved in the war in Europe.

Still, President Woodrow Wilson's successful reelection campaign of 1916 featured the slogan: "He Kept Us Out of War." As late as January of 1917, when Wilson addressed Congress, he spoke ardently of his vision of "peace without victory." Within days of the President's speech, however, Germany resumed unrestricted submarine warfare. Several unarmed American merchant vessels were sunk enroute to Europe. These attacks enflamed America's smouldering patriotic fervor and made neutrality untenable. On April 2, 1917, a shaken Wilson again addressed Congress with the famous words: "Neutrality is no longer feasible or desirable where the peace of the world is involved...the world must be safe for democracy."

Until Wilson spoke these fateful words, American popular music had, like the rest of American society, tried to ignore the European situation. Once America declared war on April 6, 1917, Tin Pan Alley began turning out new patriotic gems like George M. Cohan's "Over There" with regularity. The War songs covered a wide range of emotions that reflected the changing moods on the

home front. Initially, the nation was united by cocky patriotism: "You Can't Stop the Yanks (Till They Go Right Thru)." When the reality of the brutal War set in, this cockiness gave way to the hope that the end was near, as reflected in the hugely successful

The scholarly Woodrow Wilson preferred reading to ragtime. The President's sincere desire to keep the United States out of war was frustrated by the inability of diplomacy to control the grasping tentacles of modern warfare.

Popular songs were often used for propaganda purposes on both sides of the Rhine.

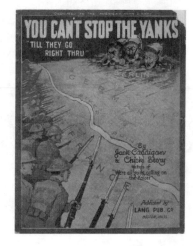

The United States' belated entry into the war and the ensuing haggling over the peace treaty broke Wilson's spirits and his health. He suffered a massive stroke in October of 1919 but, thanks to his wife's skills as a presidential proxy, Wilson remained in office until the end of his term in 1921. He died in 1924.

Four different recordings of "Just a Baby's Prayer at Twilight (For Her Daddy Over There)" reached the top ten in 1918. By far the most popular of these was by the Canadian-born tenor Henry Burr. His record held on to the number one position for eleven weeks, making it the number two hit of the decade and the number thirty recording of the first half of the century.

This short-skirted Marie, flirtatiously exposing her petticoats, was exactly the type of sexy Frenchwoman that every worried mother would have warned her innocent doughboy about before he shipped out.

"Just a Baby's Prayer at Twilight (For Her Daddy Over There)." To combat the sadness caused by separation and loss, songs like the humorous "Wee, Wee, Marie (Will You Do Zis for Me)" gave a risqué twist to the plight of provincial American doughboys being exposed to French sophistication for the first time.

It is perhaps too romantic and simplistic a notion to say that the war alone killed the energetic ragtime era. Certainly, even without the war, the style would have, by the end of the decade, probably run out of steam. Nevertheless, the grim, sobering reality of World War I undeniably changed the ragtime generation into the Lost Generation, as some of the brightest and best of the young people on both sides of the conflict were counted among the millions who were either killed, maimed, or, at the very least, emotionally scarred for life by the carnage of the trenches. The jazzy

Women's fashions changed dramatically during the 1910s. The floor-length skirts, petticoats, bulky undergarments, and long hair that were popular at the turn of the century gave way to a sleeker, more natural look suited to the ragtime era. Influential trend setters included the bobbed dancer Irene Castle and the glamorous images of the first movie stars.

Roaring Twenties recaptured some of the earlier, ragtime spirit but it just wasn't the same. The world had changed. The new responsibilities of being a modern super power had ended the United State's isolationism for good. For the almost five million veterans who had participated in the War, the experience "over there" would never be forgotten. Their care-free innocence had been another casualty of the muddy trenches. Despite the sobering effect of Prohibition, the Roaring Twenties would certainly be a party for many Americans but, unlike the Ragtime era, the mood would be one of escapism rather than confidence in the inevitable progress of modern American life.

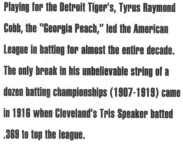

Playing for the Detroit Tiger's, Tyrus Raymond Cobb, the "Georgia Peach," led the American League in batting for almost the entire decade. The only break in his unbelievable string of a dozen batting championships (1907-1919) came in 1916 when Cleveland's Tris Speaker batted .389 to top the league.

Jim Thorpe was an All-American football player at Carlisle University. He also played major league baseball with the New York Giants. In the 1912 Olympic Games held at Stockholm Thorpe won both the decathlon and the pentathlon events but charges of professionalism later forced him to give back his gold medals. In 1955, two years after Thorpe's death, the N.F.L. Players Association established the Jim Thorpe Trophy to be awarded to pro football's most valuable player.

The Russian Revolution was one of the epic events of the 1910s that forced the United States to end its policy of isolationism in foreign affairs. Nikolai Lenin, leader of the Bolsheviks, overthrew the Czar on November 6, 1917.

After You've Gone

Registration 8
Rhythm: Swing

By Creamer and Layton

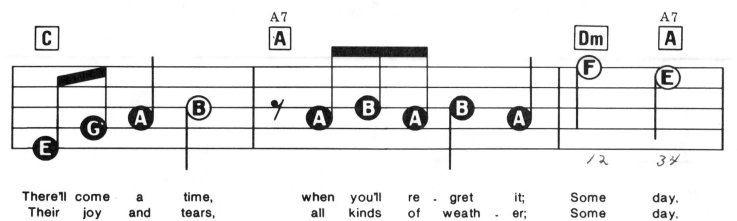

There'll come a time, when you'll re - gret it; Some day,
Their joy and tears, all kinds of weath - er; Some day,

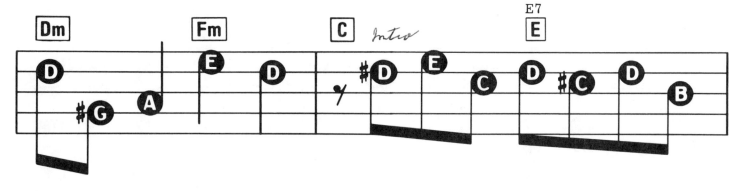

when you grow lone - ly, Your heart will break like mine and
blue and down heart - ed, You'll long to be with me right

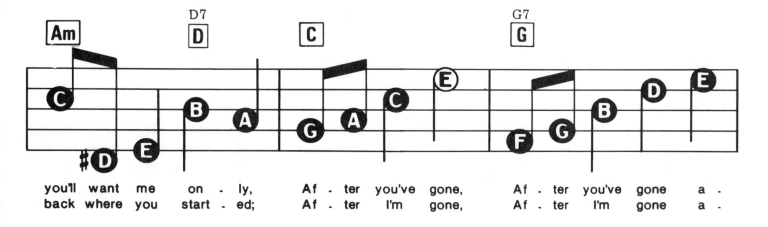

you'll want me on - ly, Af - ter you've gone,
back where you start - ed; Af - ter I'm gone, Af - ter I'm gone a -

Af - ter you've gone a -

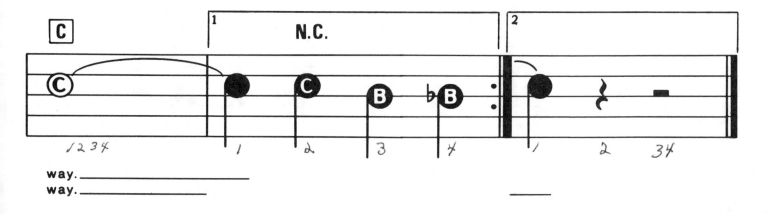

way. _____
way. _____

Alexander's Ragtime Band

Registration 5
Rhythm: Fox Trot or Swing

Words and Music by
Irving Berlin

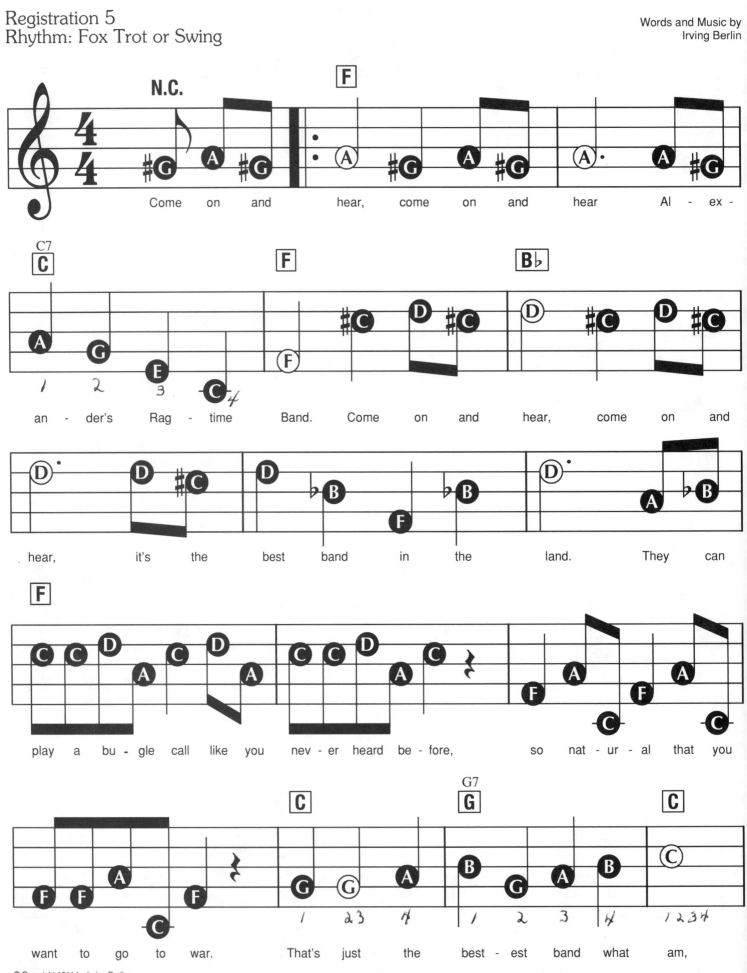

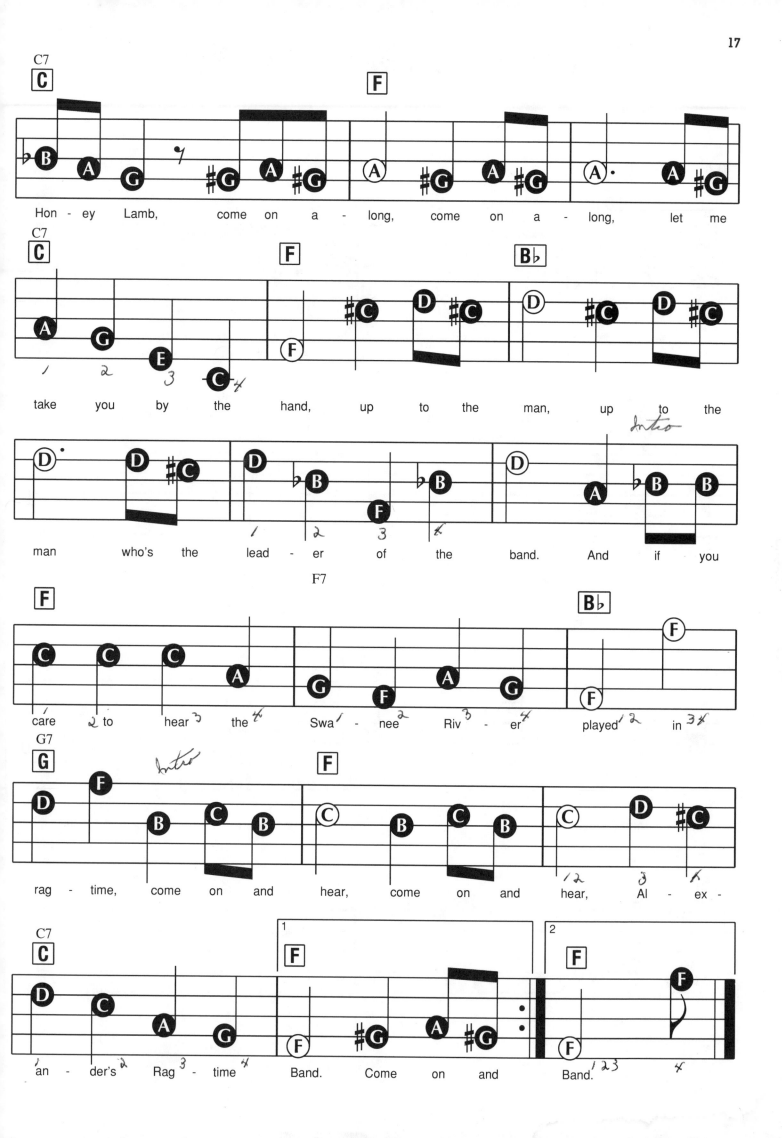

Art Is Calling For Me

Registration 3
Rhythm: March

Music by Victor Herbert
Lyrics by Harry B. Smith

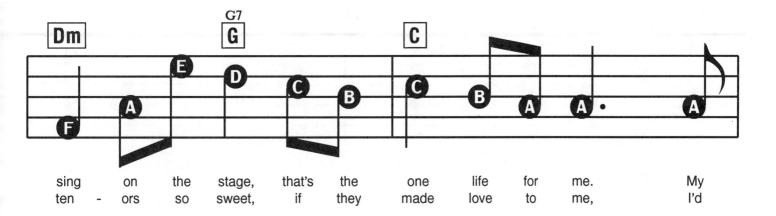

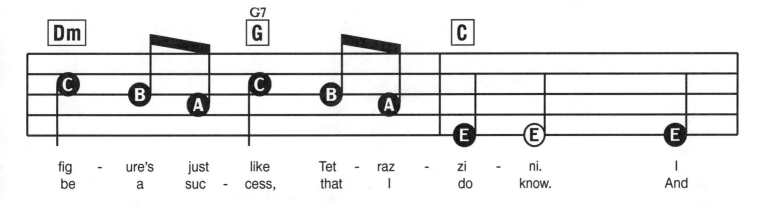

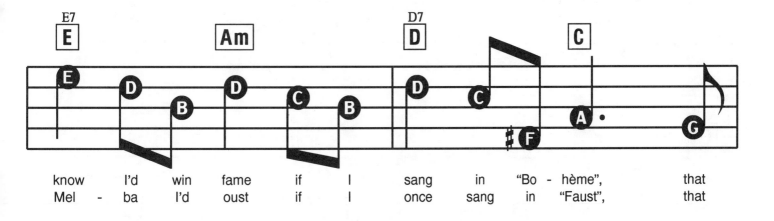

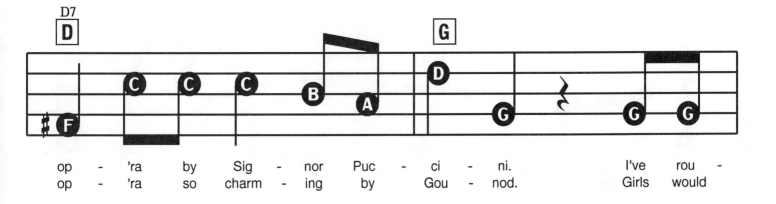

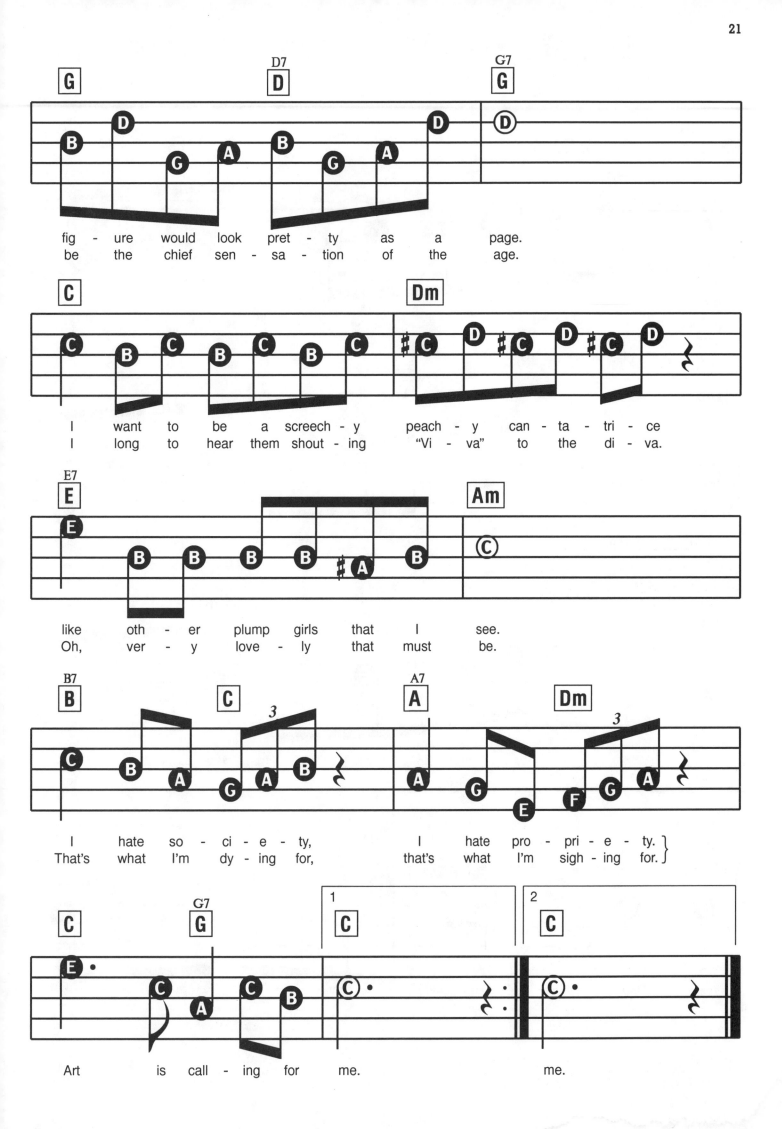

Ah! Sweet Mystery Of Life

Registration 3
Rhythm: Fox Trot or Ballad

Music by Victor Herbert
Lyrics by Rida Johnson Young

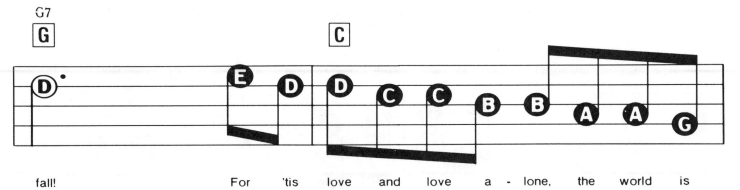

fall!   For 'tis love and love a - lone, the world is

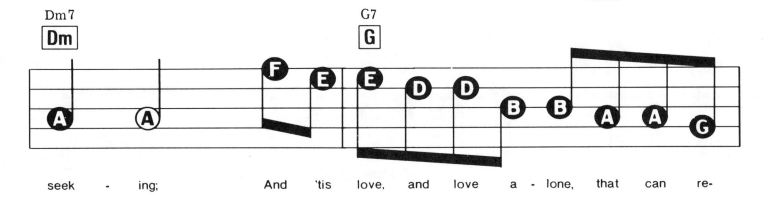

seek - ing;   And 'tis love, and love a - lone, that can re-

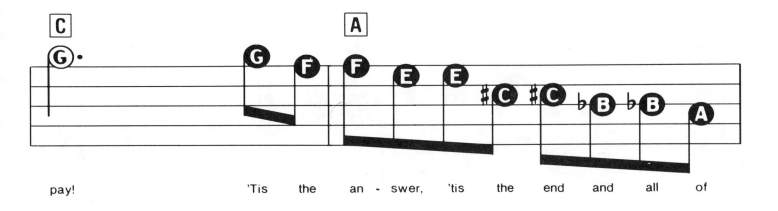

pay!   'Tis the an - swer, 'tis the end and all of

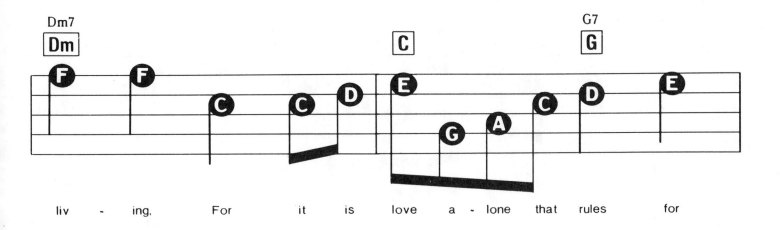

liv - ing, For it is love a - lone that rules for

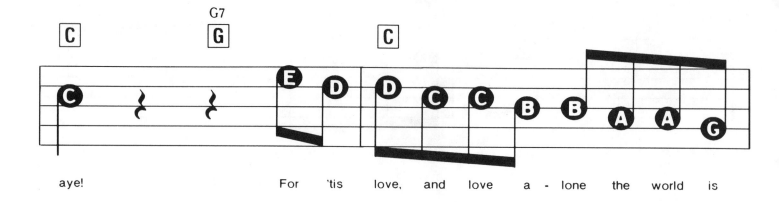

aye!   For 'tis love, and love a - lone the world is

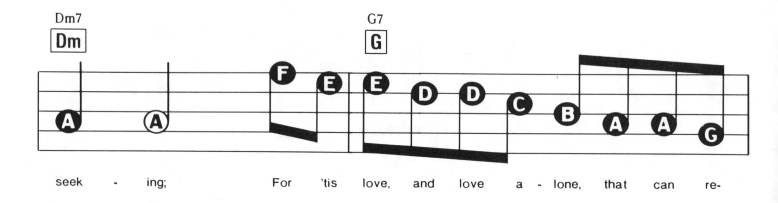

seek - ing;   For 'tis love, and love a - lone, that can re-

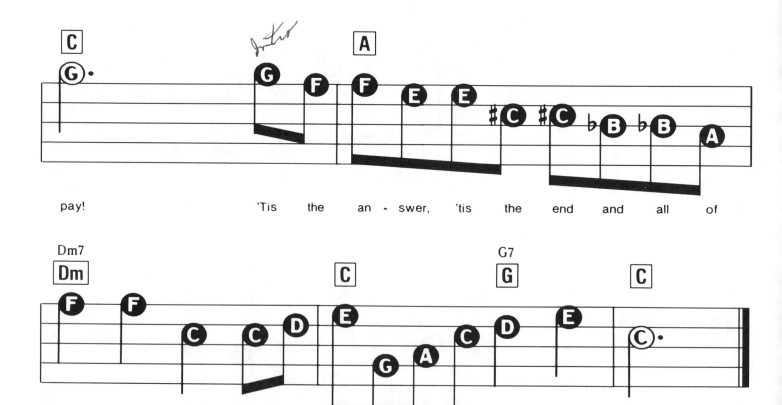

pay!   'Tis the an - swer, 'tis the end and all of

liv - ing,   For it is love a - lone that rules for   aye!

Be My Little Baby Bumble Bee

Registration 10
Rhythm: March

Words by Stanley Murphy
Music by Henry I. Marshall

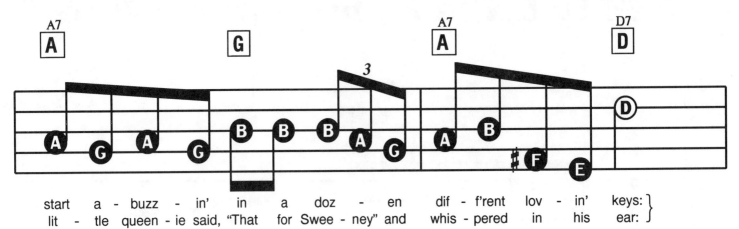

start a - buzz - in' in a doz - en dif - f'rent lov - in' keys:
lit - tle queen - ie said, "That for Swee - ney" and whis - pered in his ear:

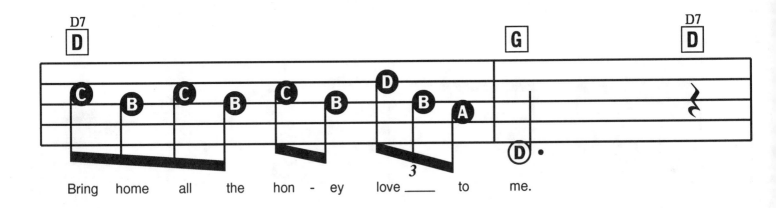

Be my lit - tle ba - by bum - ble bee.

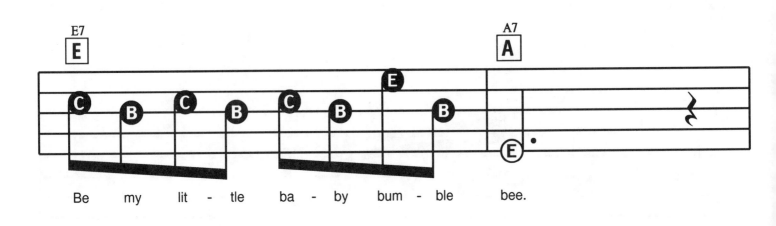

Bring home all the hon - ey love ____ to me.

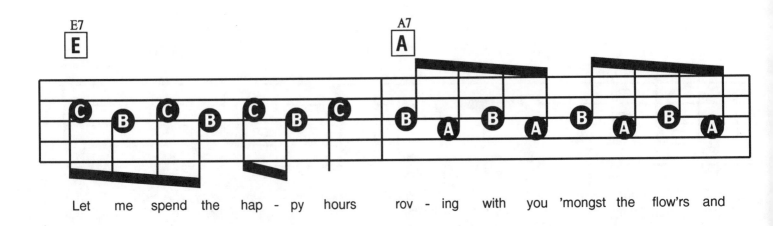

Let me spend the hap - py hours rov - ing with you 'mongst the flow'rs and

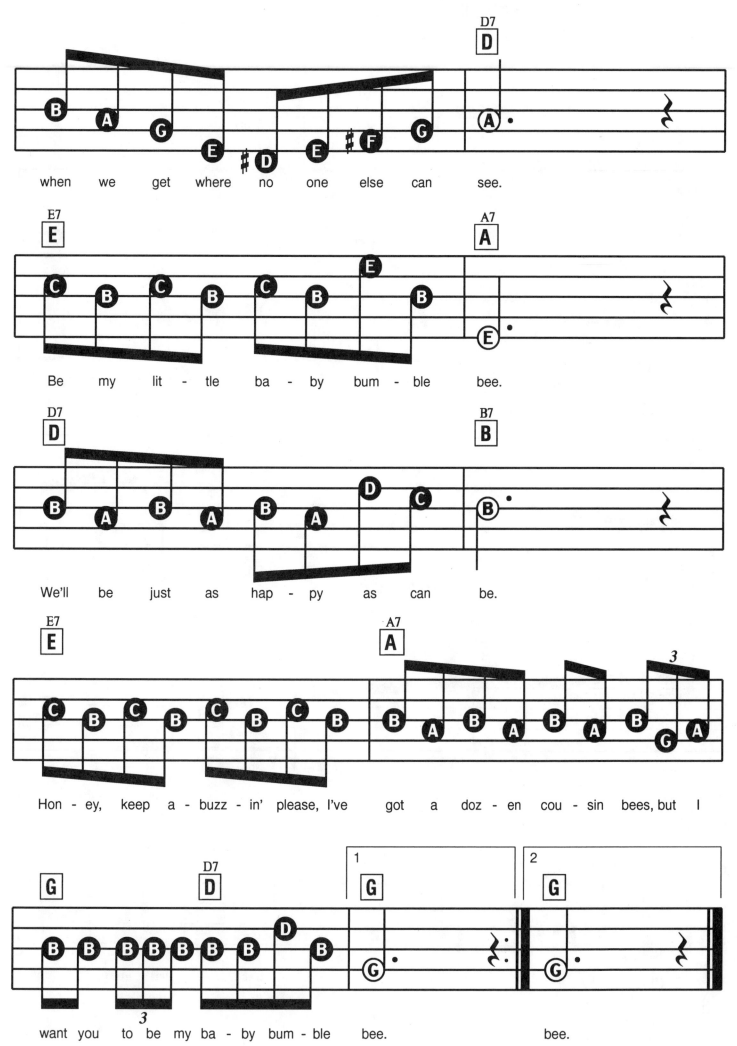

Ballin' The Jack

Registration 9
Rhythm: Swing or Fox Trot

Words by Jim Burris
Music by Chris Smith

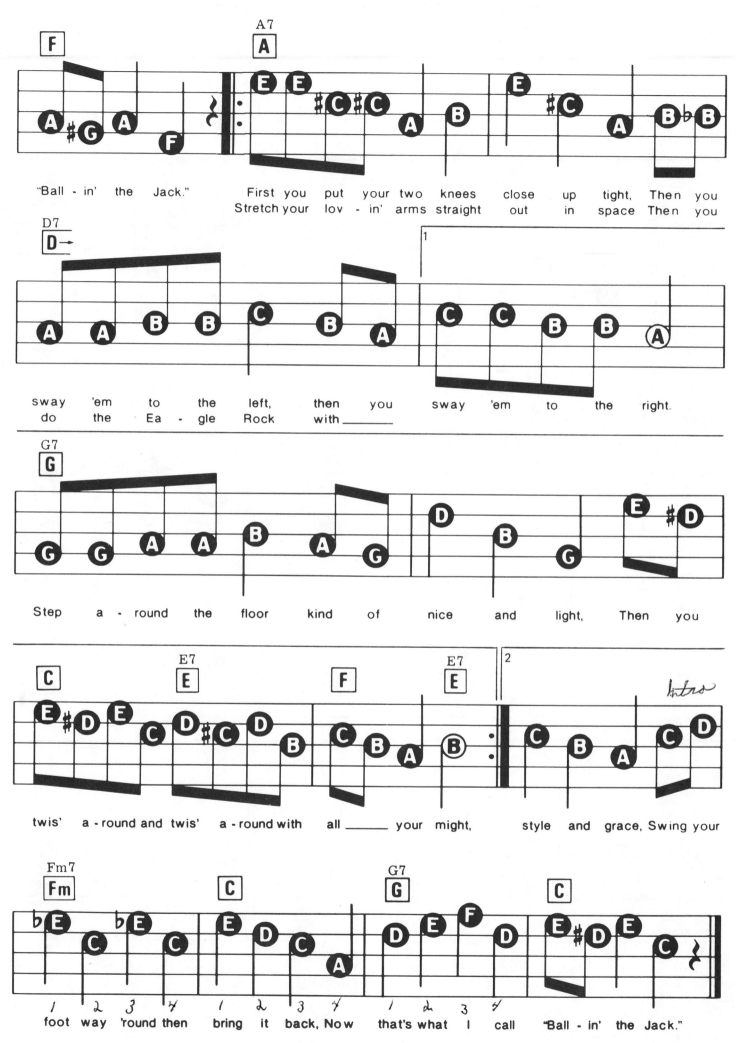

The Bells Of St. Mary's

Registration 4
Rhythm: Fox Trot or Swing

Words by Douglas Furber
Music by Emmett Adams

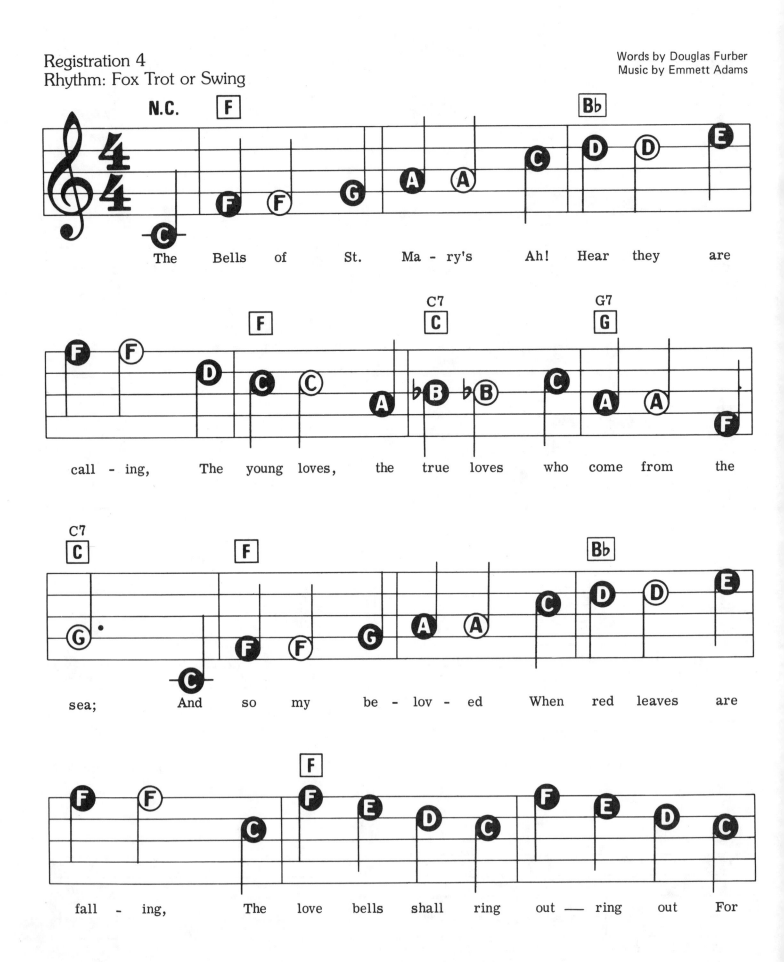

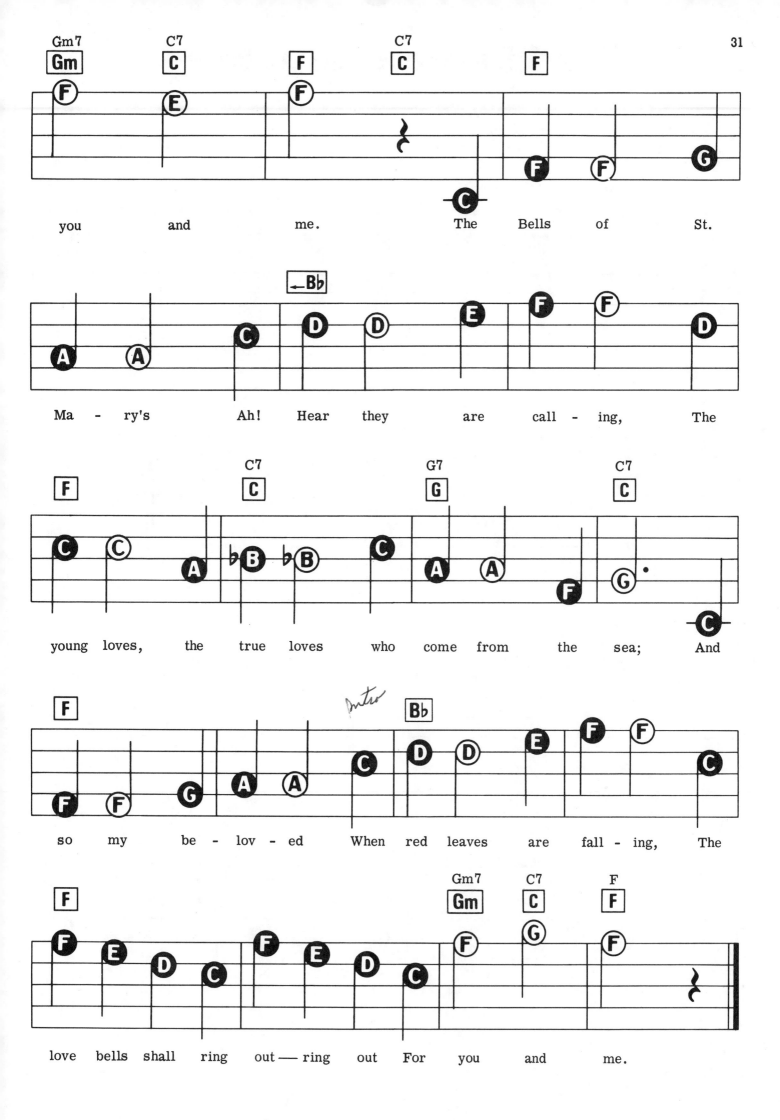

By The Beautiful Sea

Registration 2
Rhythm: Ballad

Words by Harold R. Atteridge
Music by Harry Carroll

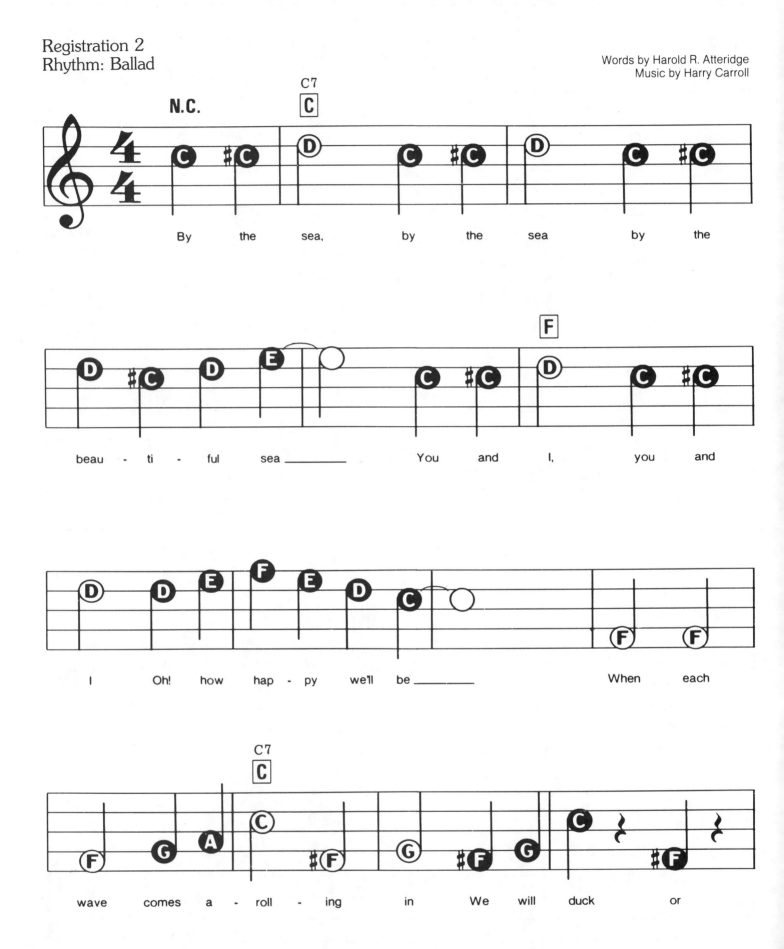

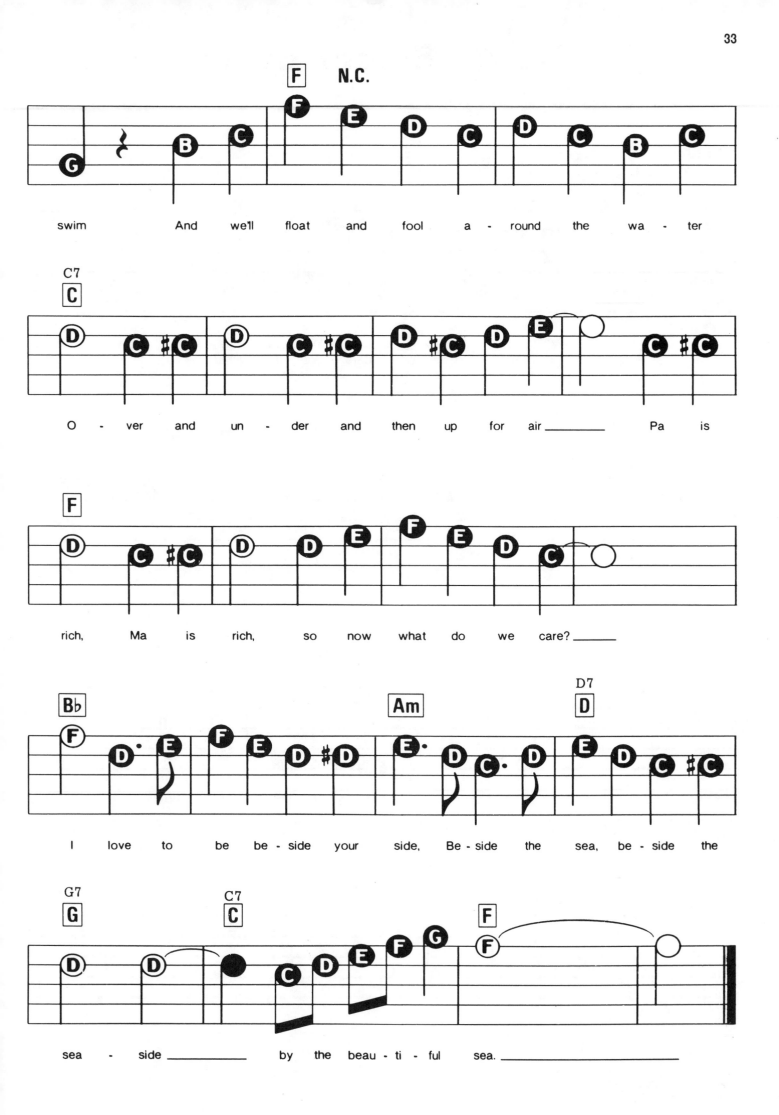

Beale Street Blues

Registration 4
Rhythm: March

Words and Music by
W.C. Handy

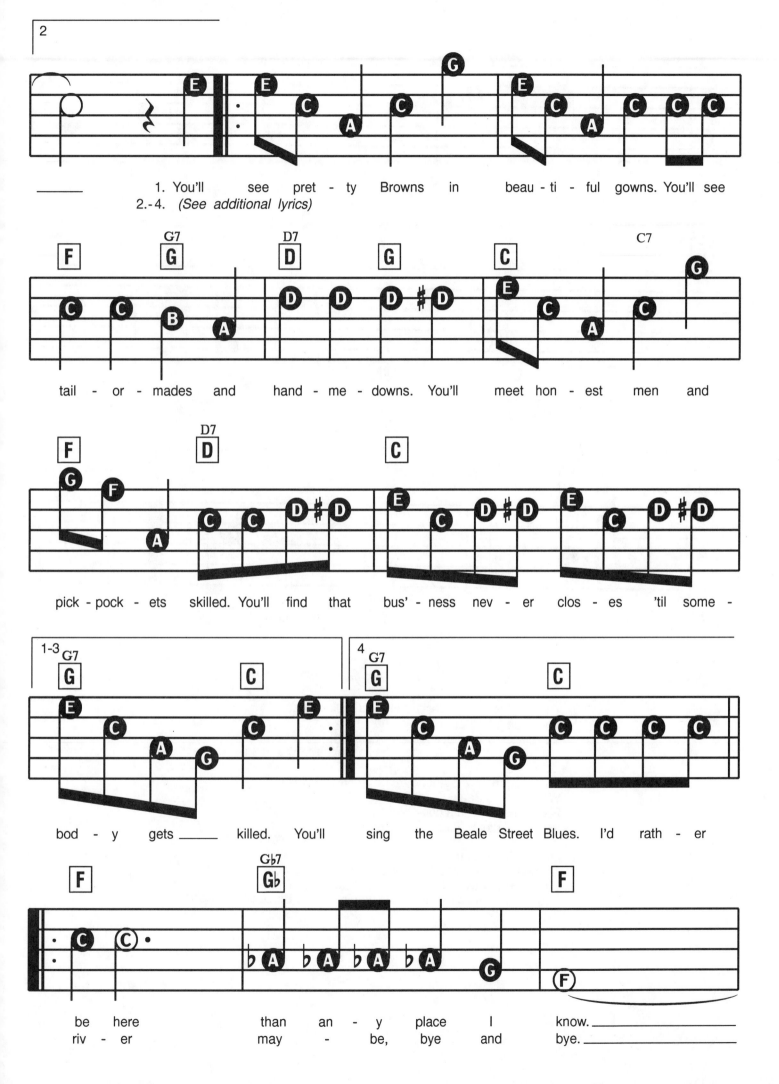

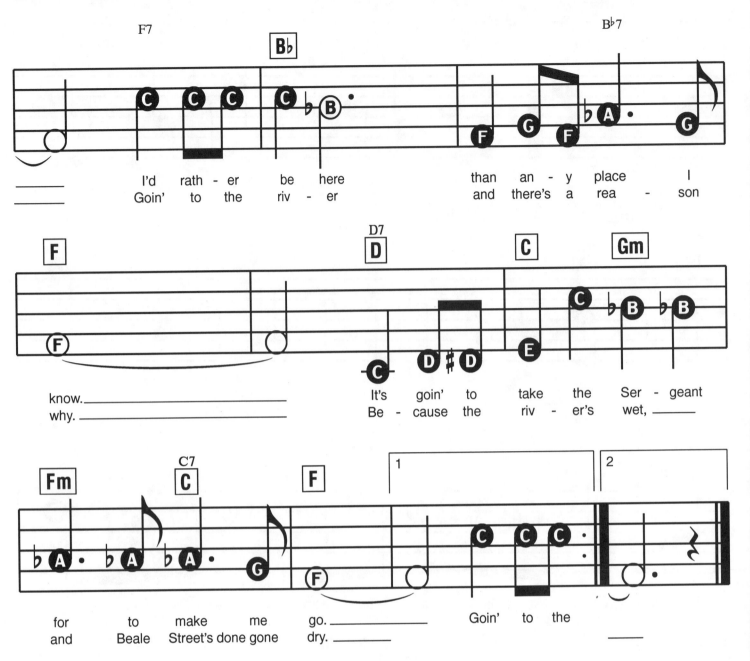

Additional Lyrics

2. You'll see Hog Nose rest'rants and Chitlin' Cafes.
   You'll see jugs that tell of bygone days
   And places once places now just a sham.
   You'll see Golden Balls enough to pave the New Jerusalem.

3. You'll see men who rank with the first in the nation
   Who come to Beale for inpiration.
   Politicians call you a dub unless you've been initiated
   In the Rickriters Club.

4. If Beale Street could talk, if Beale Street could talk,
   Married men would have to take their beds and walk,
   Except one or two who never drank booze,
   And the blind man on the corner who sings the Beale Street Blues.

Come, Josephine In My Flying Machine
(Up She Goes!)

Registration 7
Rhythm: Waltz

Music by Fred Fischer
Words by Alfred Bryan

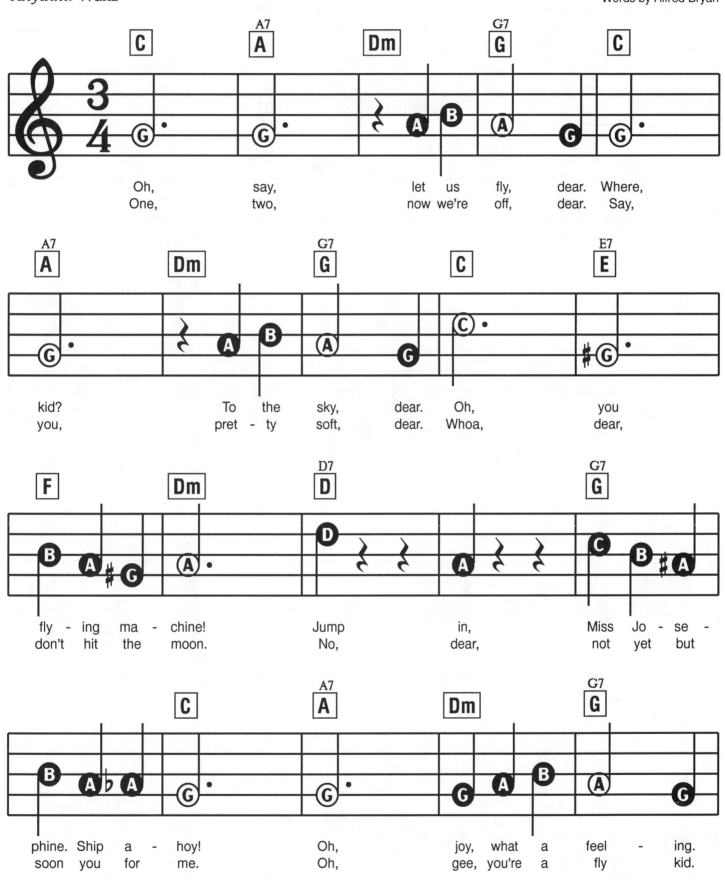

38

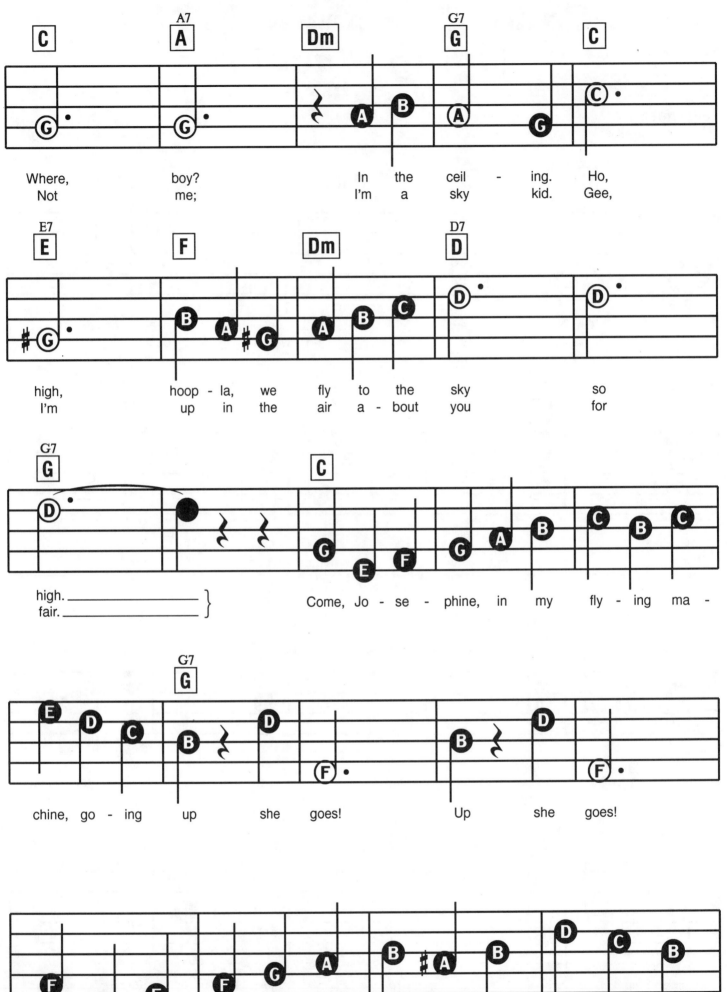

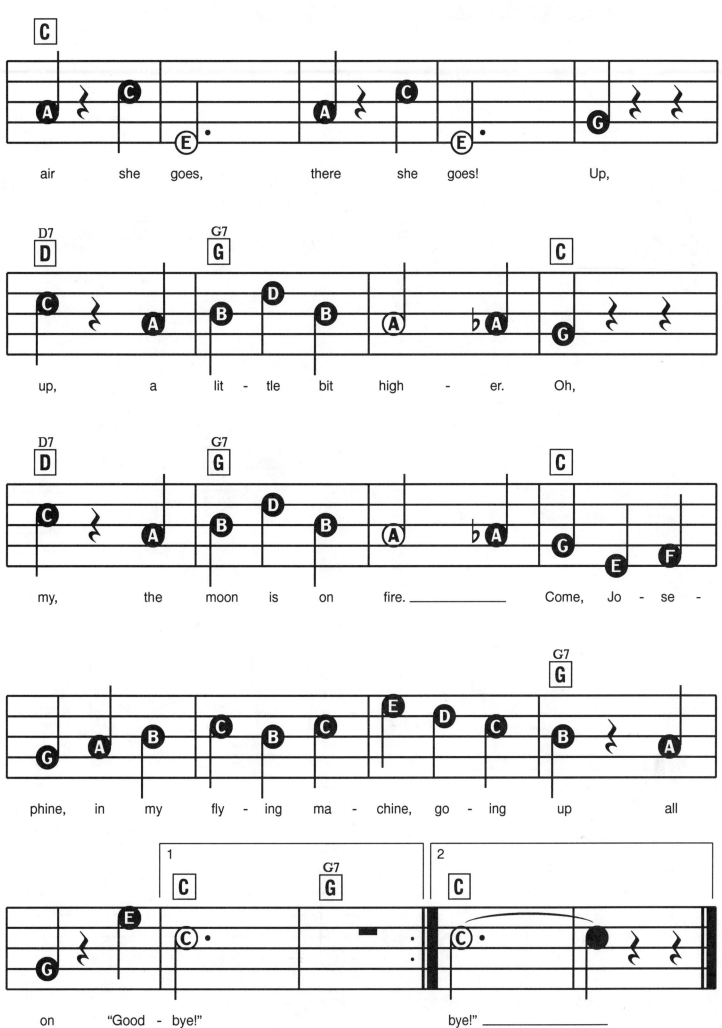

Chinatown, My Chinatown

Registration 4
Rhythm: Swing

Words by William Jerome
Music by Jean Schwartz

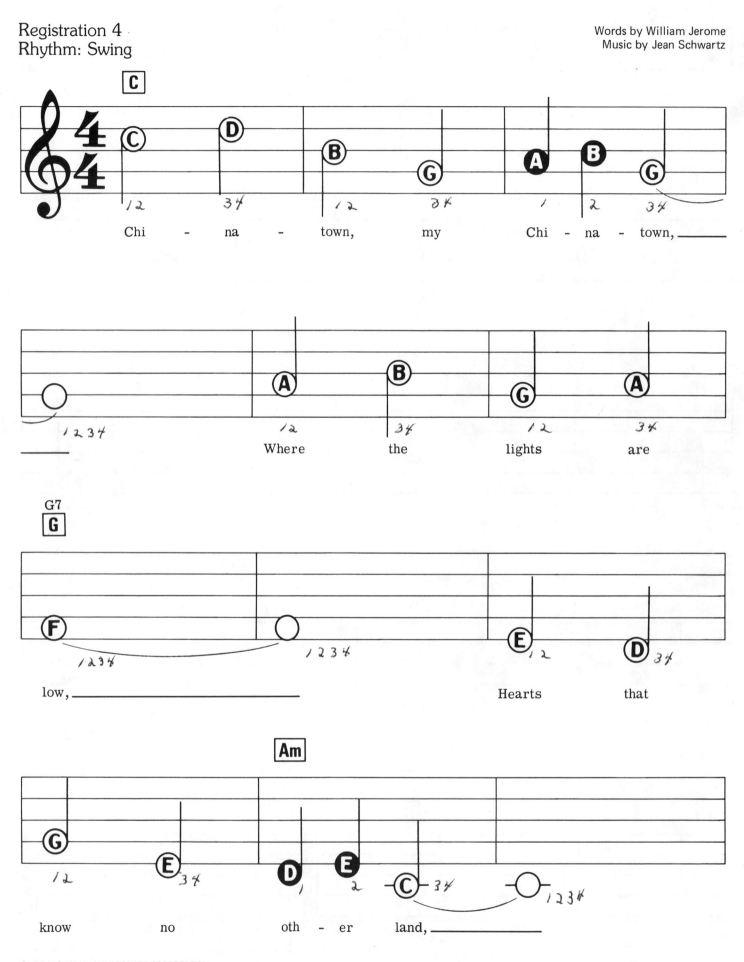

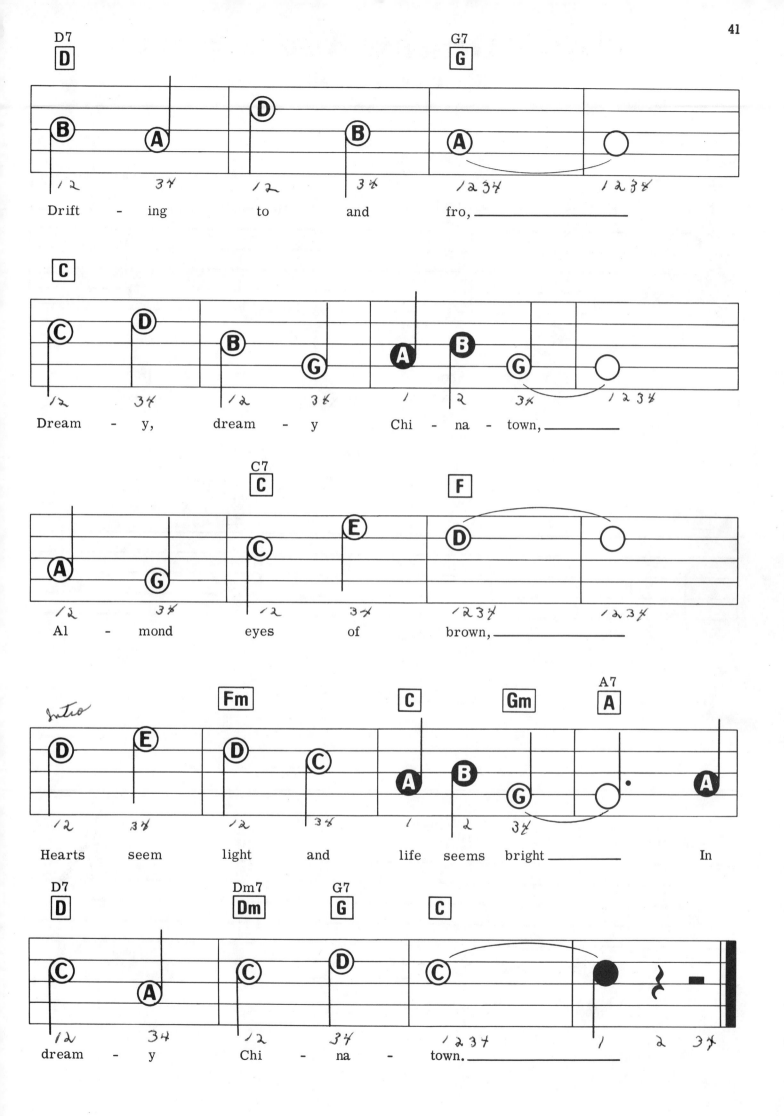

Danny Boy
(Londonderry Air)

Registration 10
Rhythm: 8-Beat or Pops

Words by
Frederick E. Weatherly

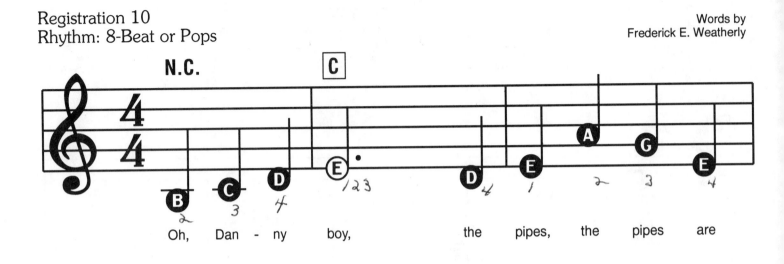

Oh, Dan - ny boy, the pipes, the pipes are

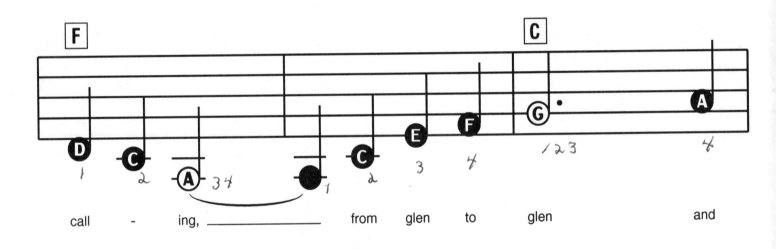

call - ing, from glen to glen and

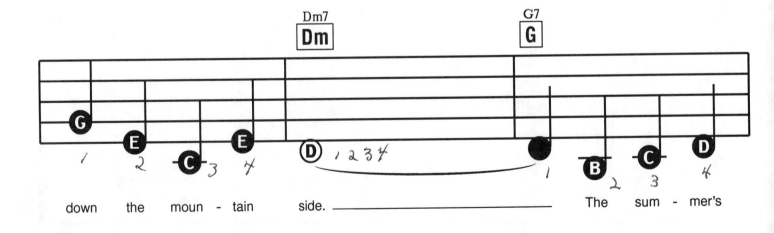

down the moun - tain side. The sum - mer's

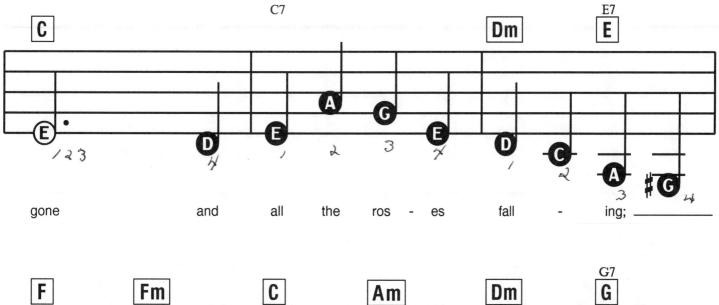

gone   and   all   the   ros - es   fall - ing; _____

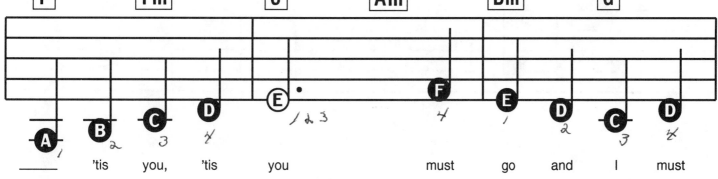

_____ 'tis   you,   'tis   you   must   go   and   I   must

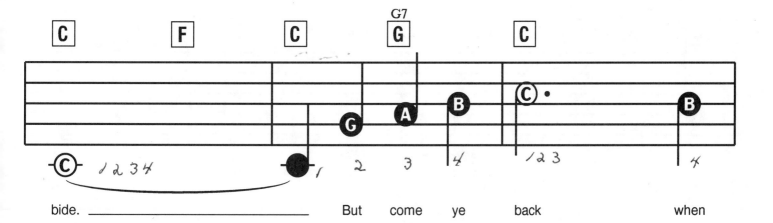

bide. _____ But   come   ye   back   when

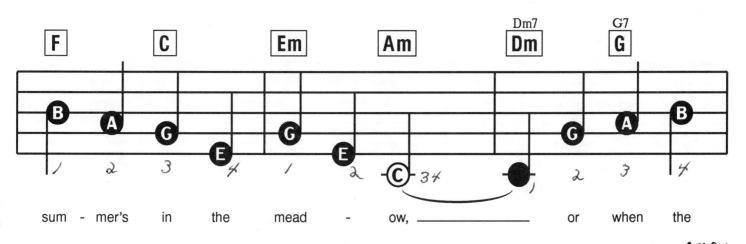

sum - mer's   in   the   mead - ow, _____ or   when   the

over

44

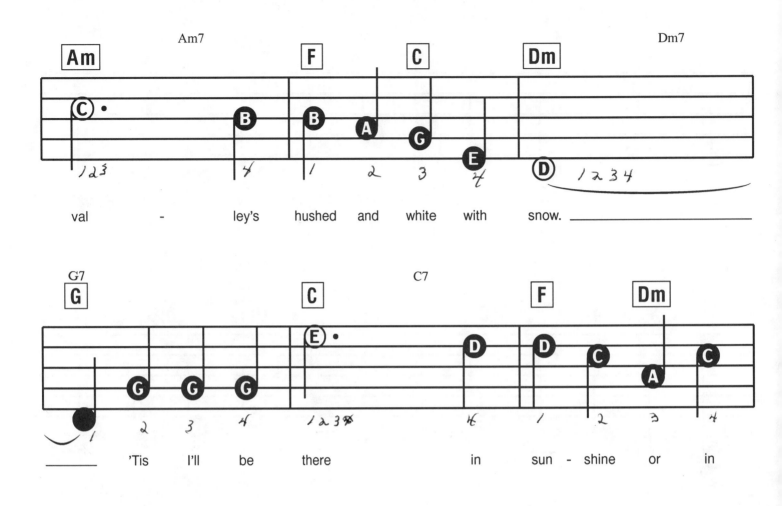

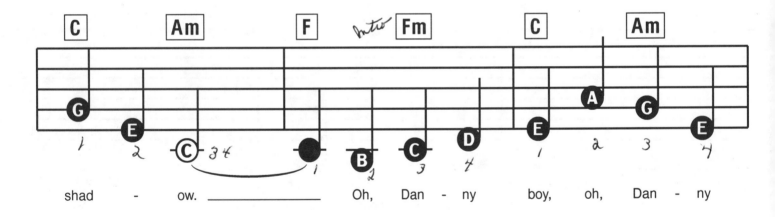

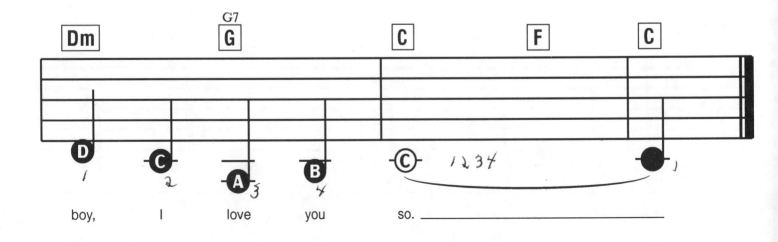

Don't Bite The Hand That's Feeding You

Registration 4
Rhythm: March

Music by Jimmie Morgan
Words by Thomas Hoier

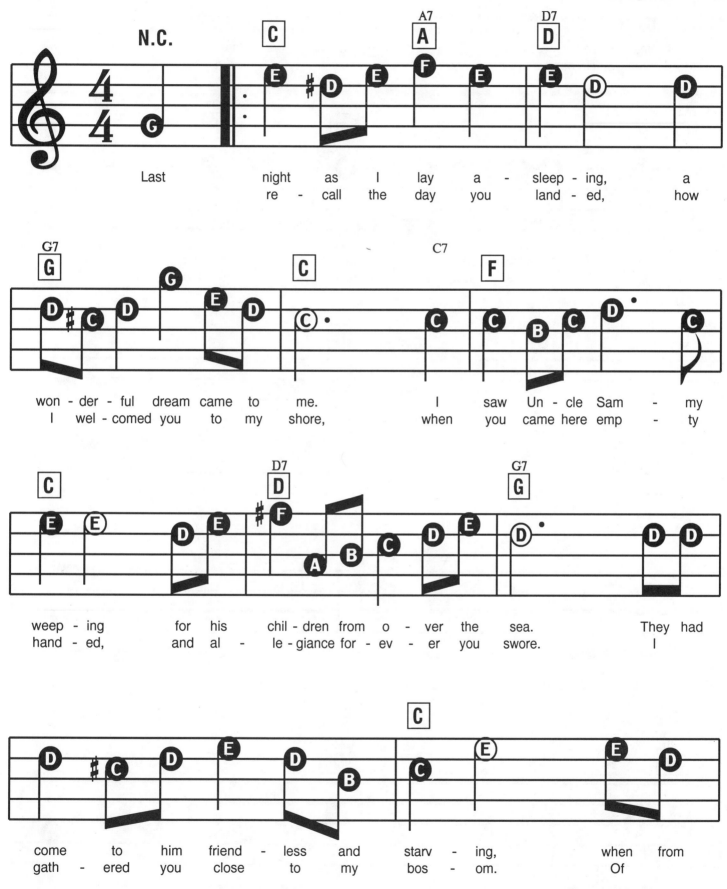

46

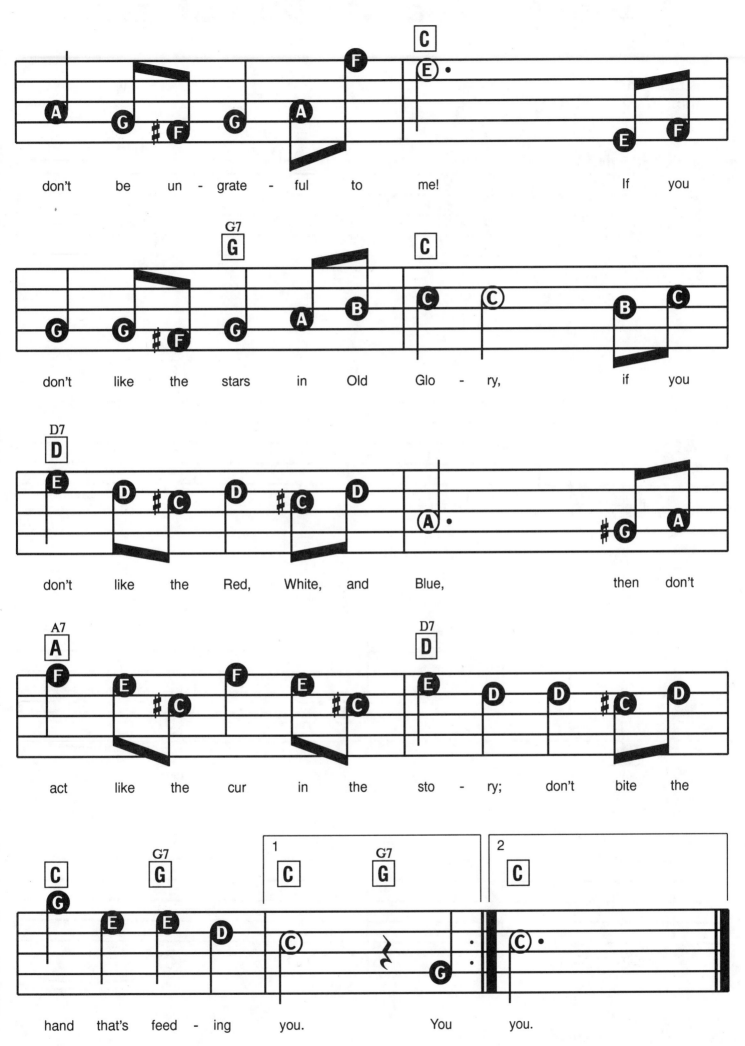

Down By The Old Mill Stream

Registration 3
Rhythm: Waltz

Words and Music by
Tell Taylor

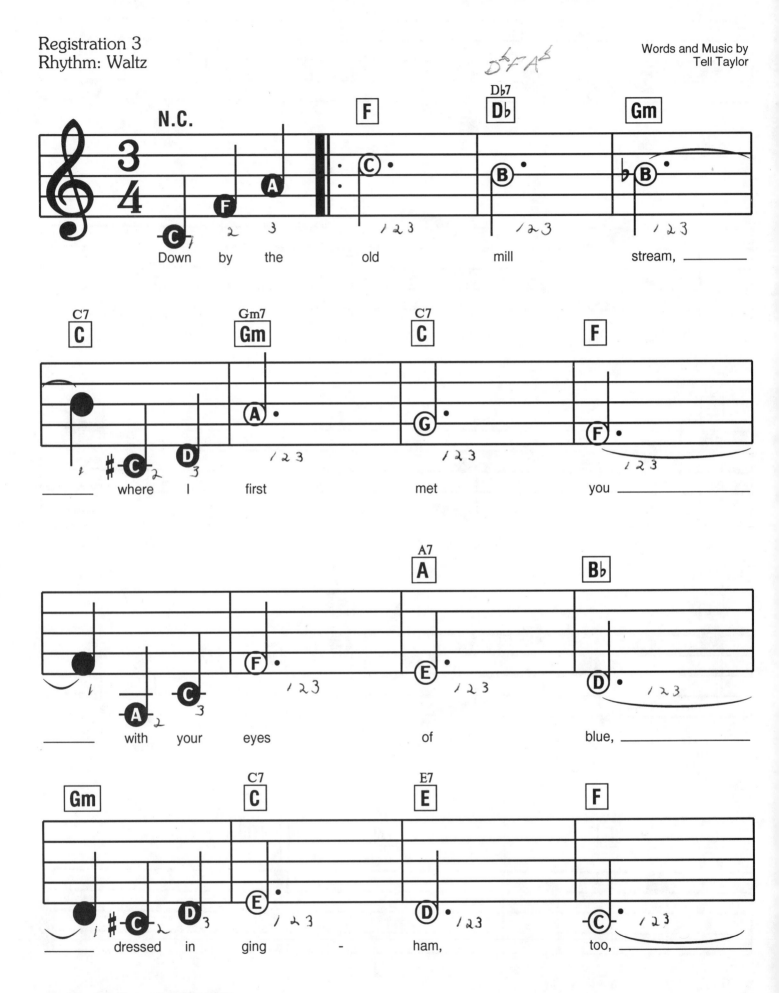

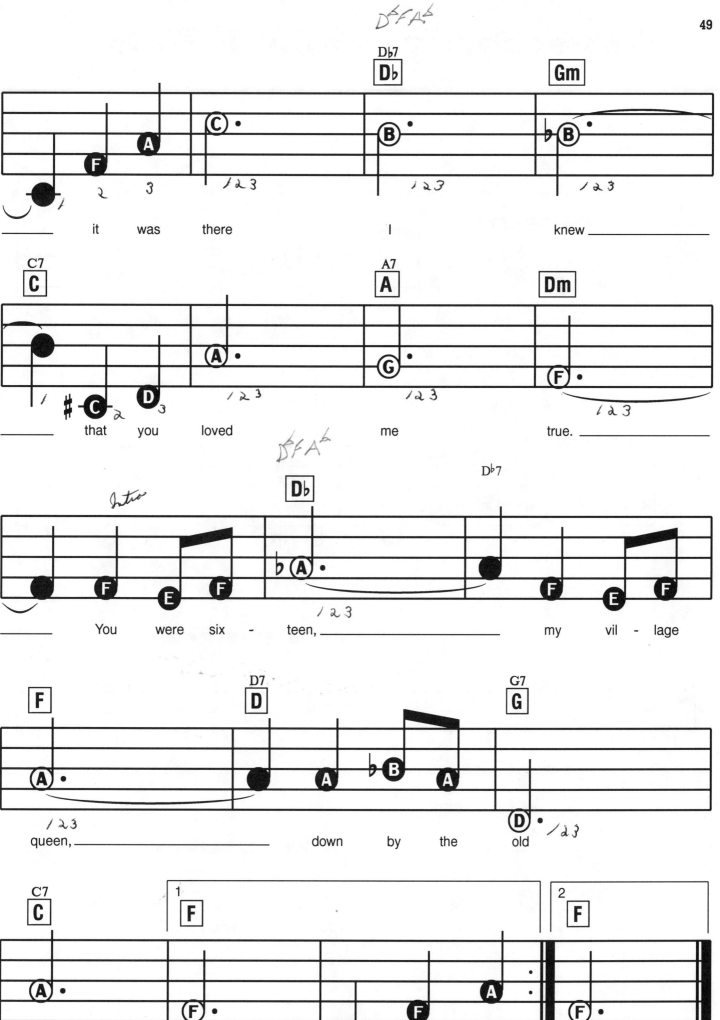

49

Everybody's Doin' It Now

Registration 8
Rhythm: Swing

Words and Music by
Irving Berlin

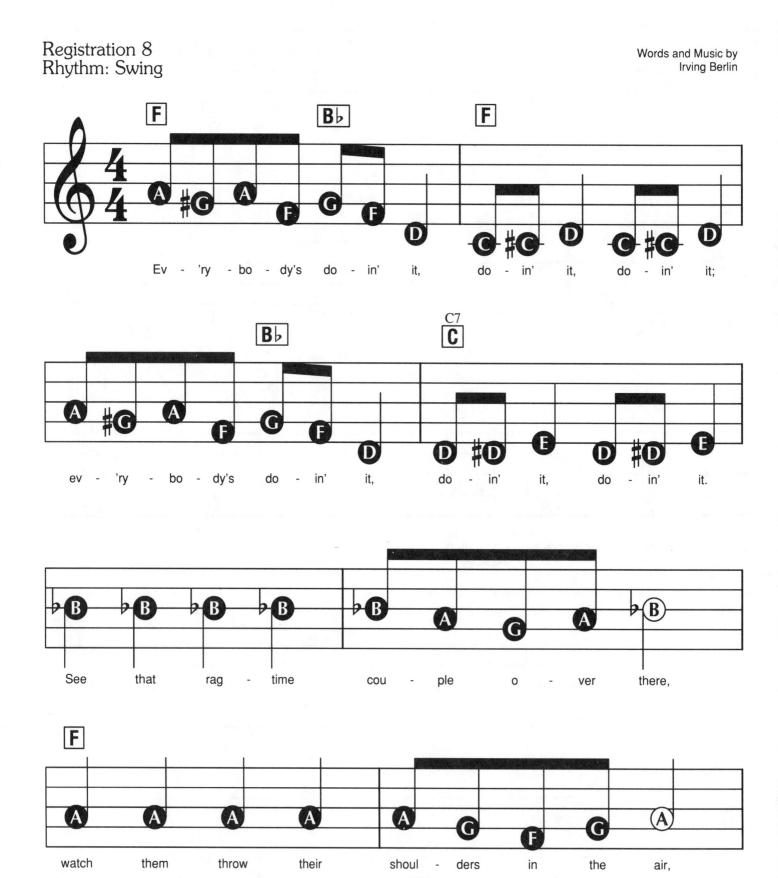

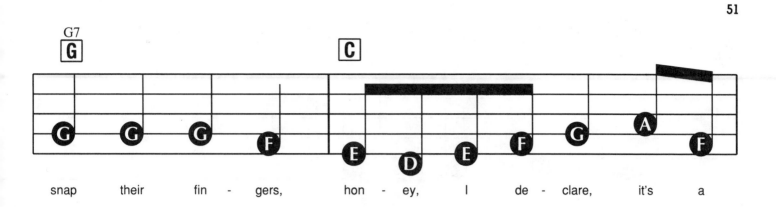

snap their fin - gers, hon - ey, I de - clare, it's a

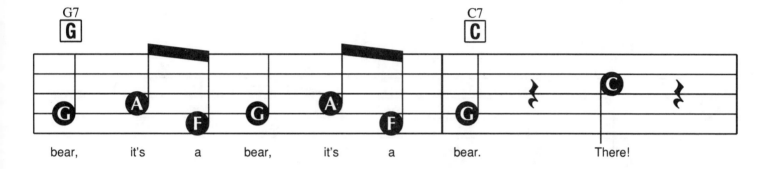

bear, it's a bear, it's a bear. There!

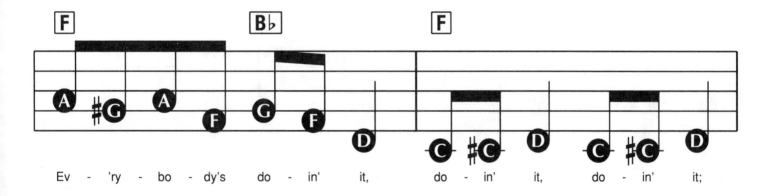

Ev - 'ry - bo - dy's do - in' it, do - in' it, do - in' it;

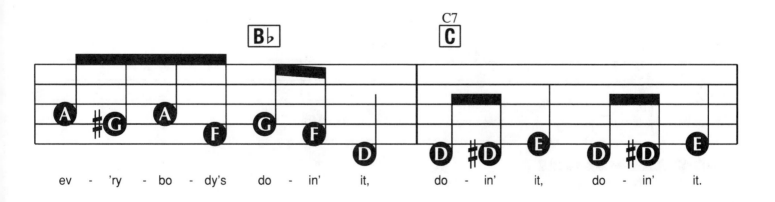

ev - 'ry - bo - dy's do - in' it, do - in' it, do - in' it.

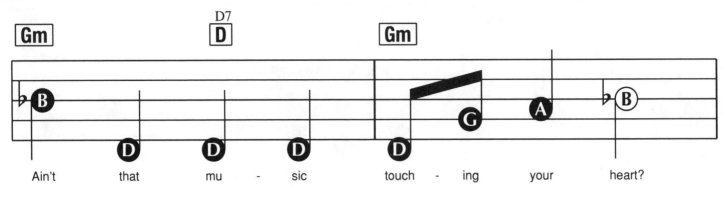

Ain't that mu - sic touch - ing your heart?

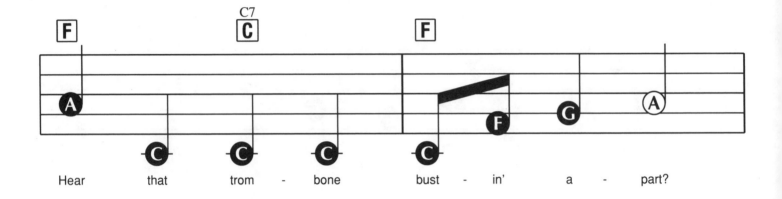

Hear that trom - bone bust - in' a - part?

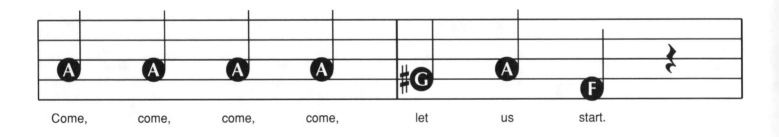

Come, come, come, come, let us start.

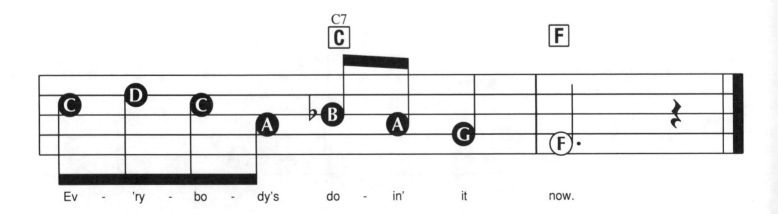

Ev - 'ry - bo - dy's do - in' it now.

Giannina Mia

Registration 5
Rhythm: Waltz

Words by Otto Harbach
Music by Rudolf Friml

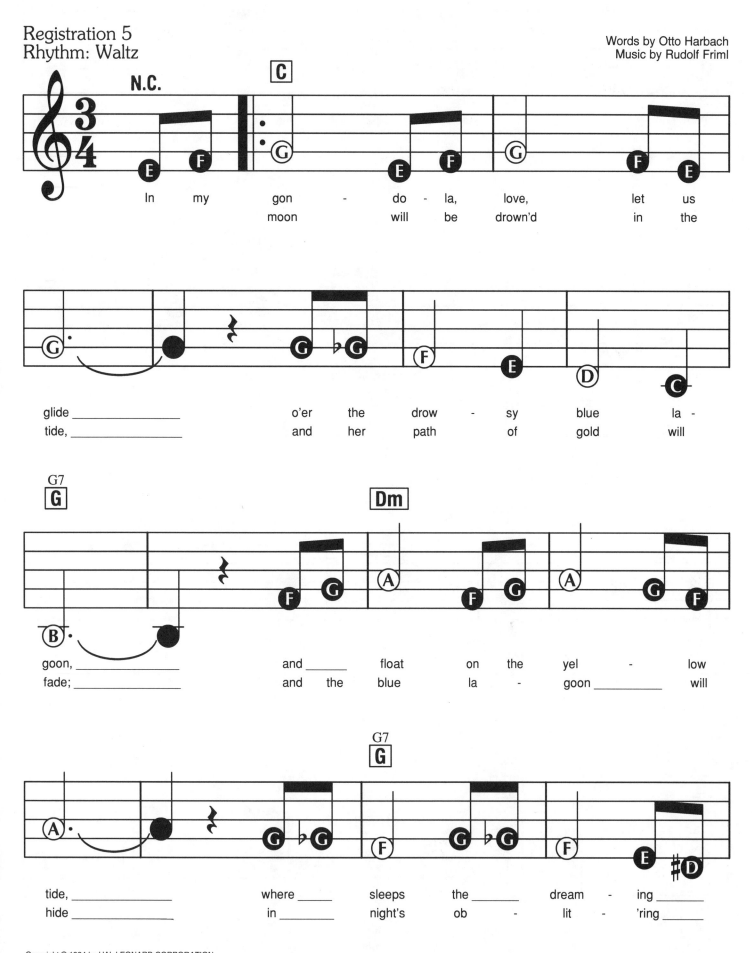

54

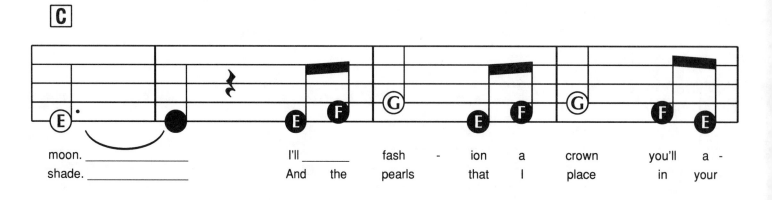

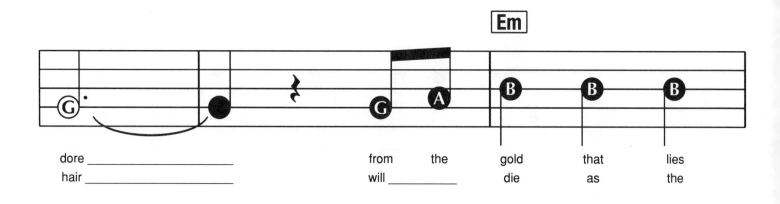

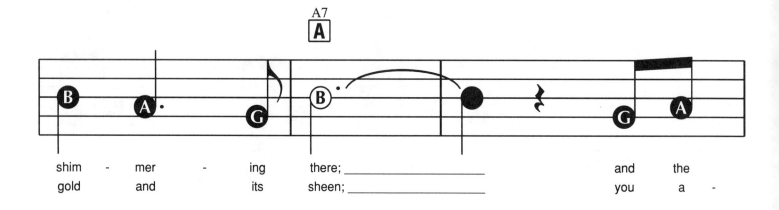

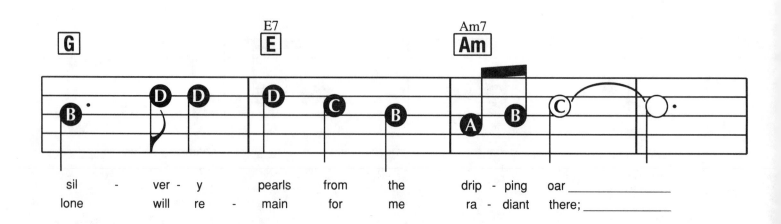

55

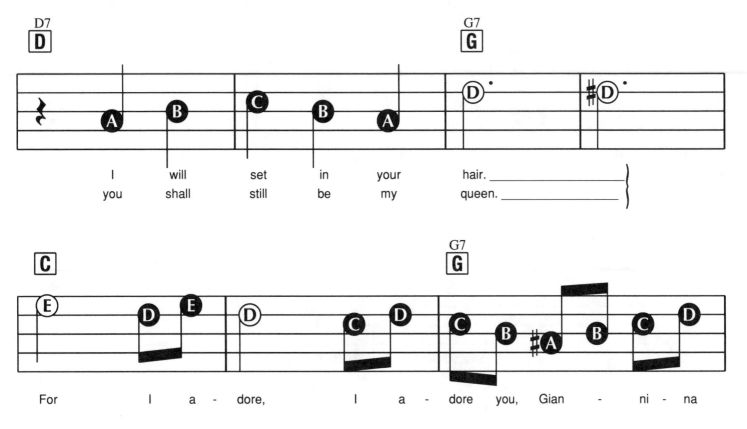

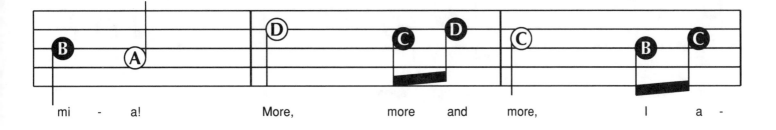

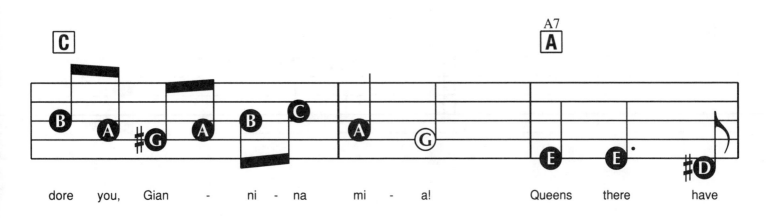

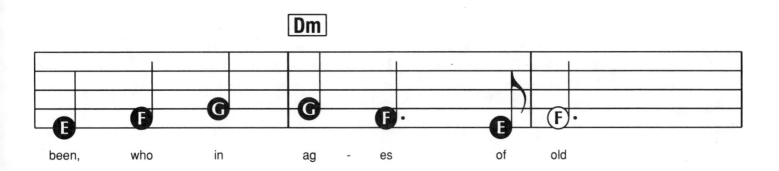

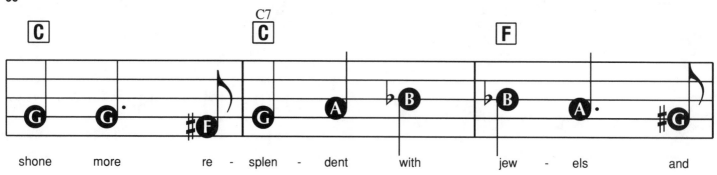

shone   more   re - splen - dent   with   jew - els   and

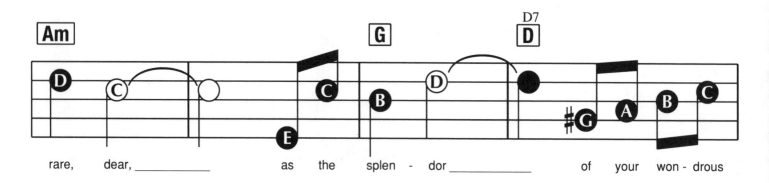

gold,   pre - cious   jew - els   not   half   so

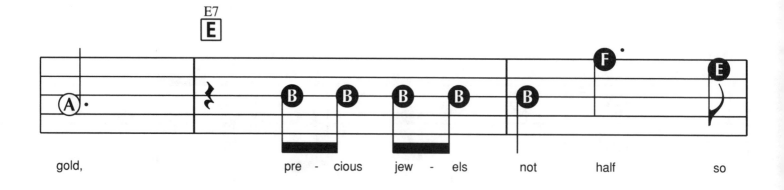

rare,   dear, _____   as   the   splen - dor _____   of   your   won - drous

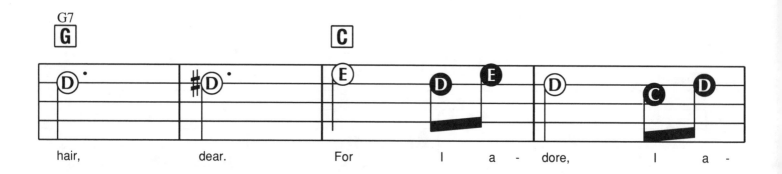

hair,   dear.   For   I   a - dore,   I   a -

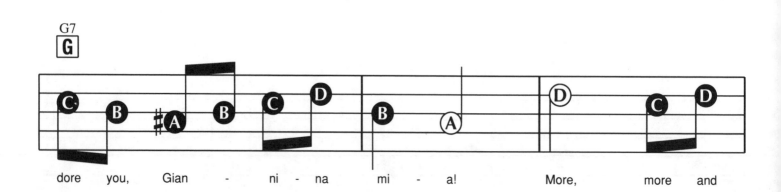

dore   you,   Gian - ni - na   mi - a!   More,   more and

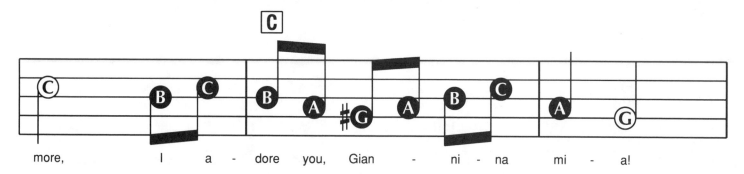

more, I a - dore you, Gian - ni - na mi - a!

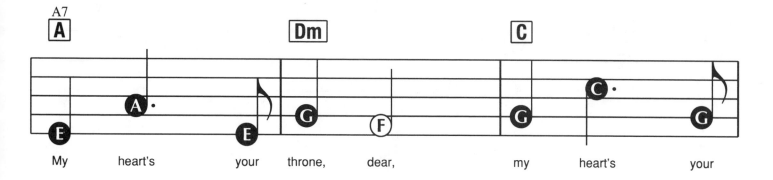

My heart's your throne, dear, my heart's your

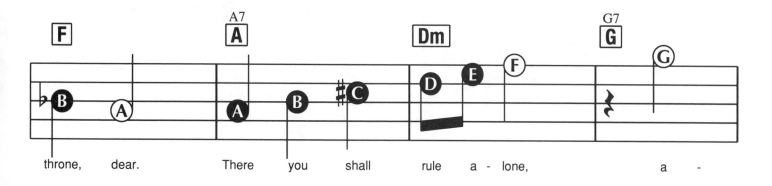

throne, dear. There you shall rule a - lone, a -

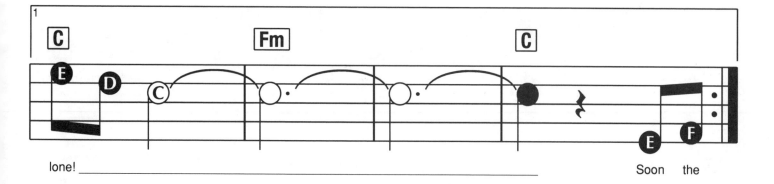

lone! _____ Soon the

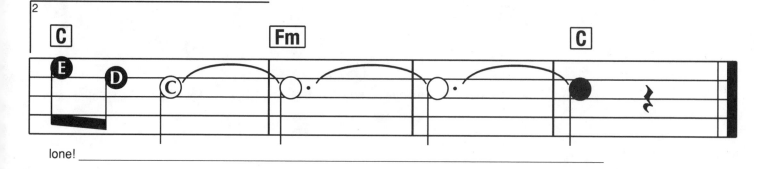

lone! _____

For Me And My Gal

Words by Edgar Leslie and E. Ray Goetz
Music by George W. Meyer

Registration 3
Rhythm: Swing

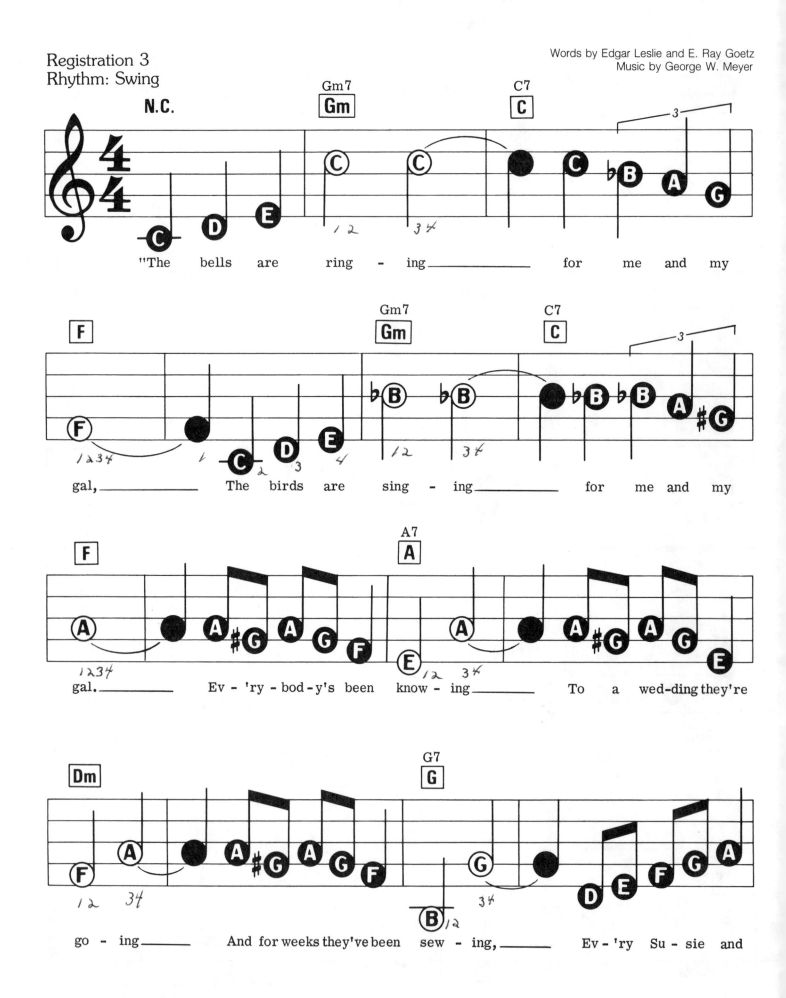

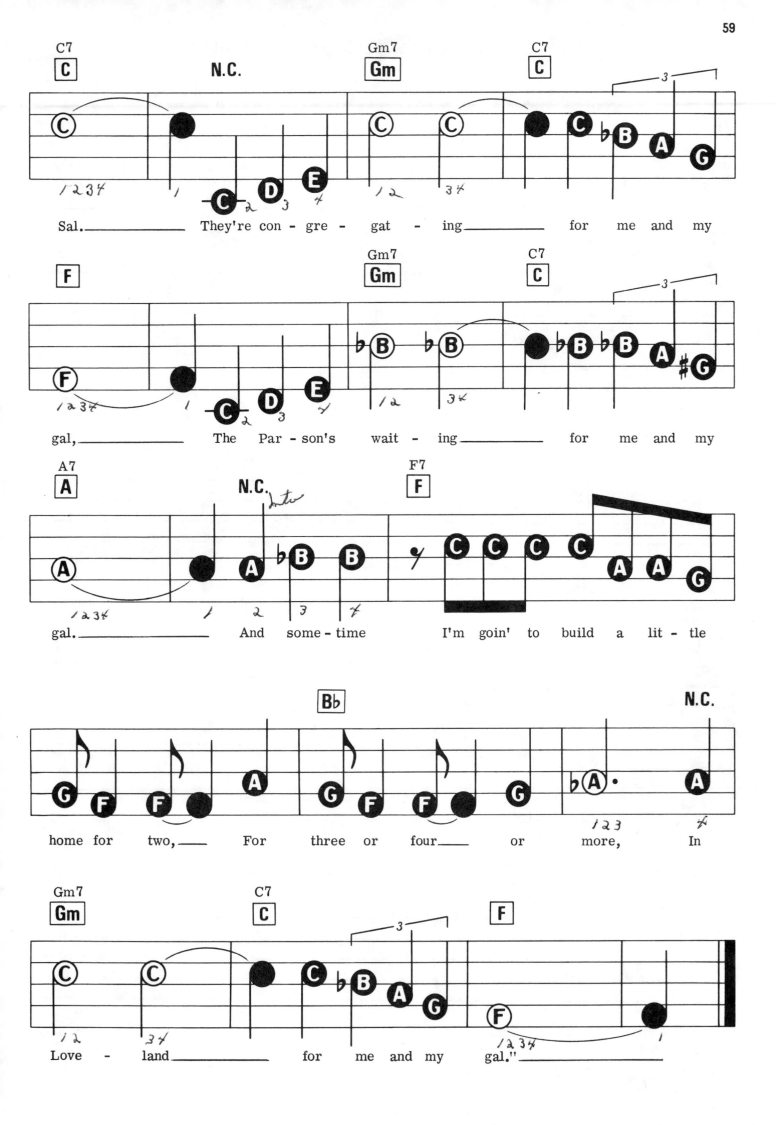

He'd Have To Get Under - Get Out And Get Under
(To Fix Up His Automobile)

Registration 4
Rhythm: March

Music by Maurice Abrahams
Words by Grant Clarke and Edgar Leslie

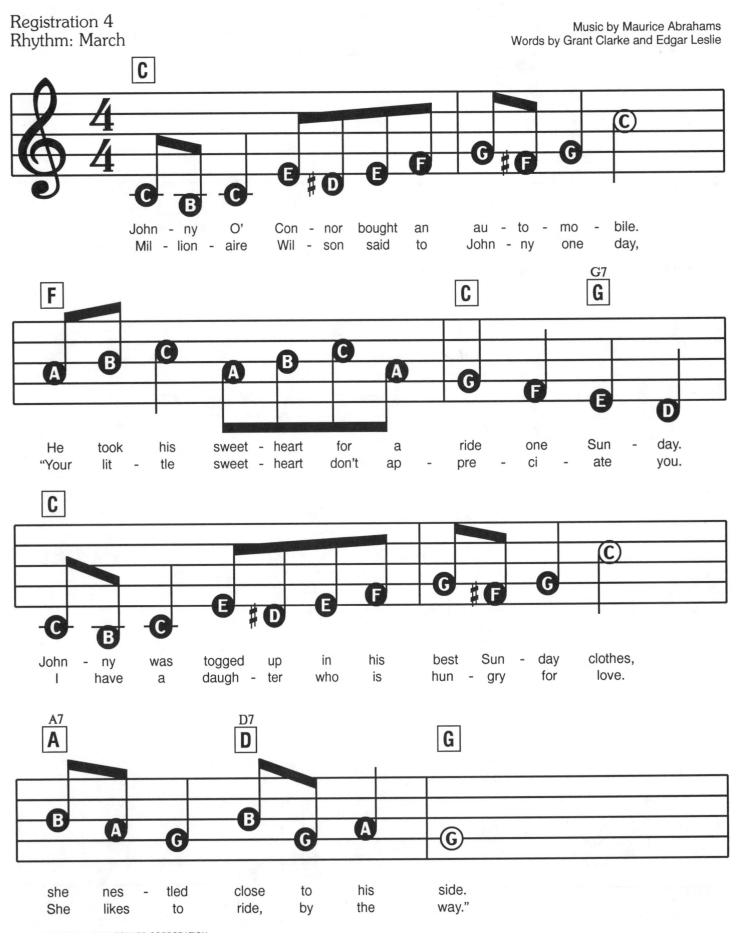

61

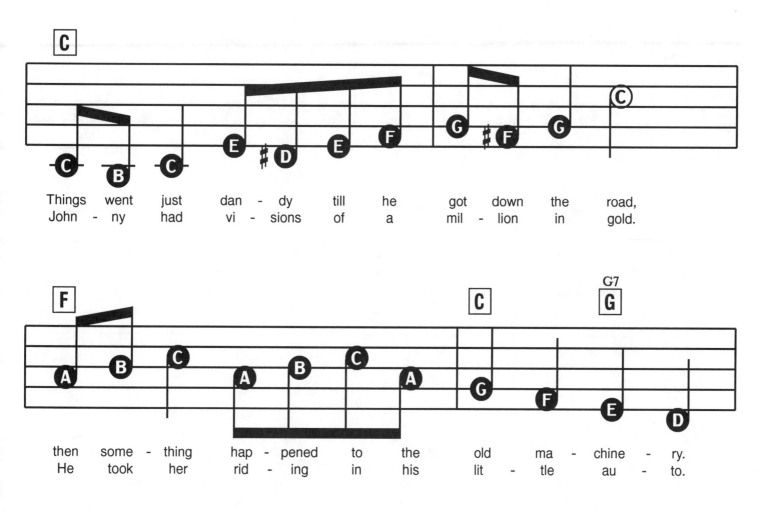

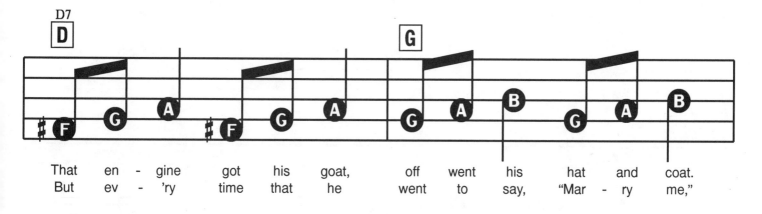

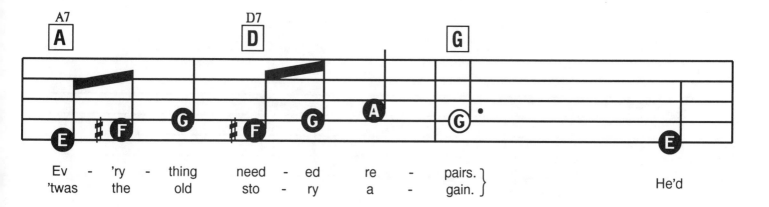

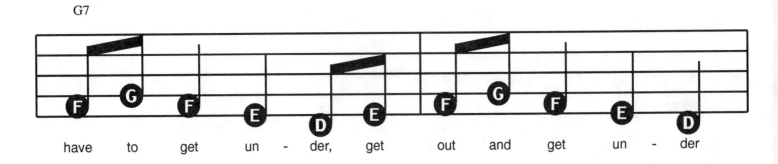

have to get un - der, get out and get un - der

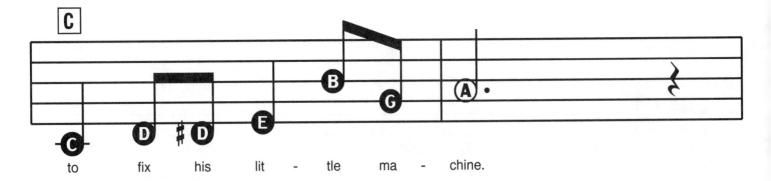

to fix his lit - tle ma - chine.

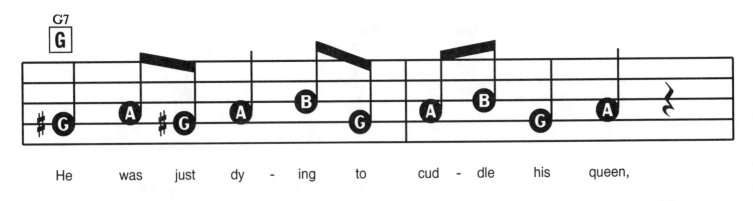

He was just dy - ing to cud - dle his queen,

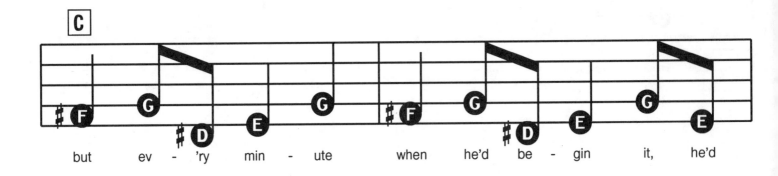

but ev - 'ry min - ute when he'd be - gin it, he'd

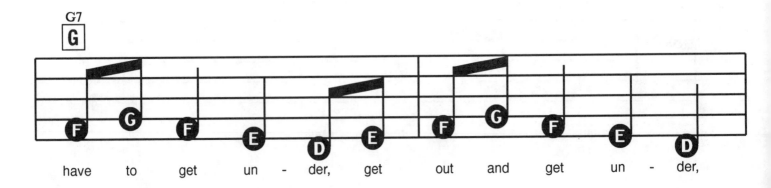

have to get un - der, get out and get un - der,

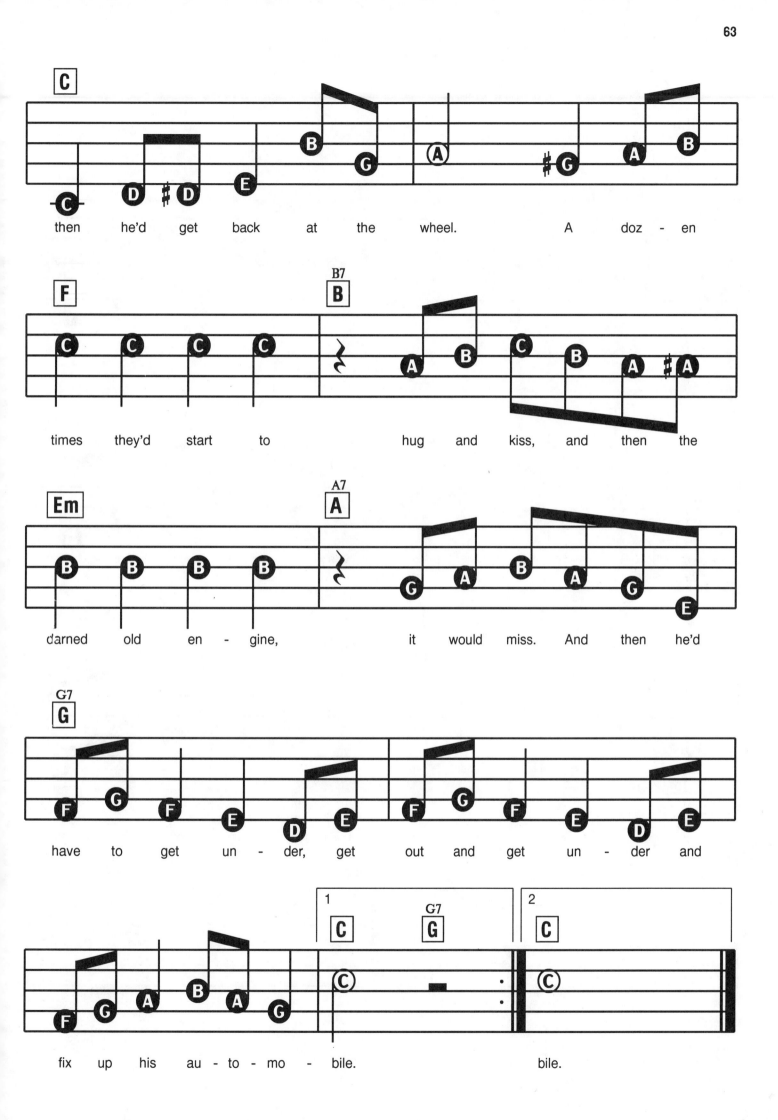

Memphis Blues

Registration 4
Rhythm: March

Words and Music by
W.C. Handy

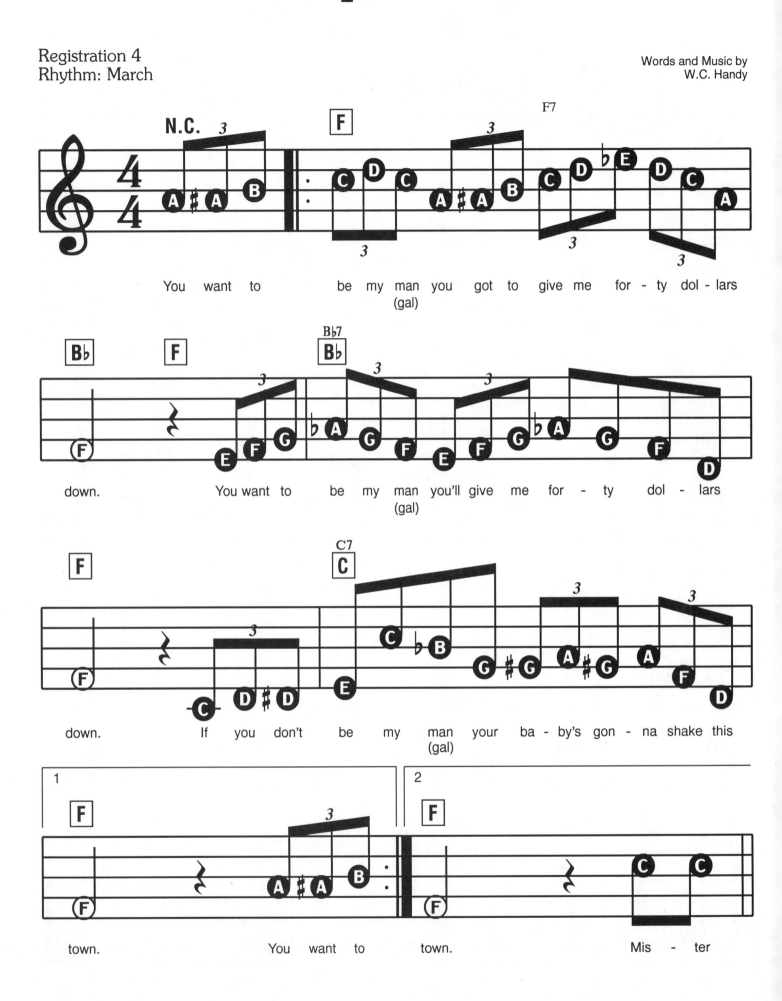

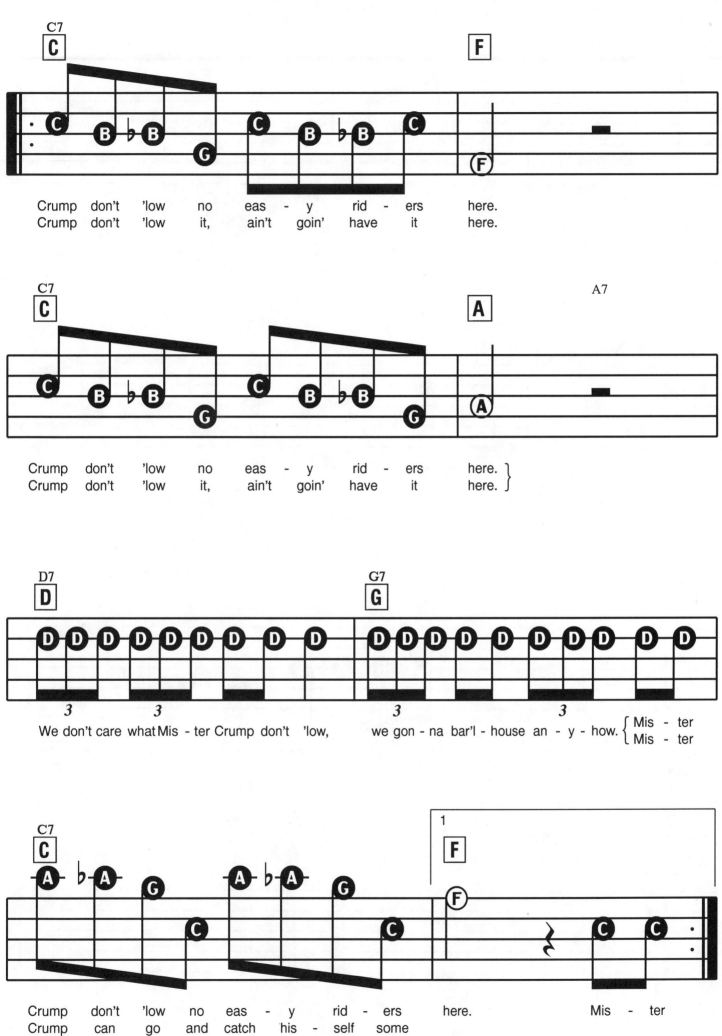

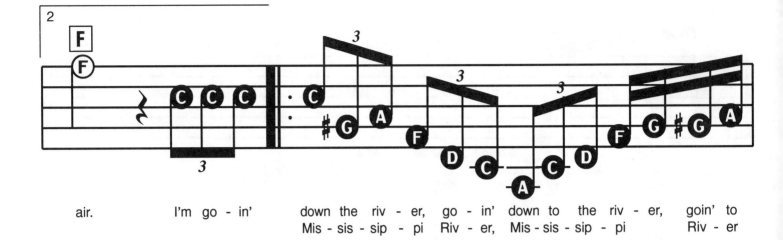

air.   I'm go - in'   down the riv - er, go - in' down to the riv - er, goin' to
Mis - sis - sip - pi River, Mis - sis - sip - pi   Riv - er

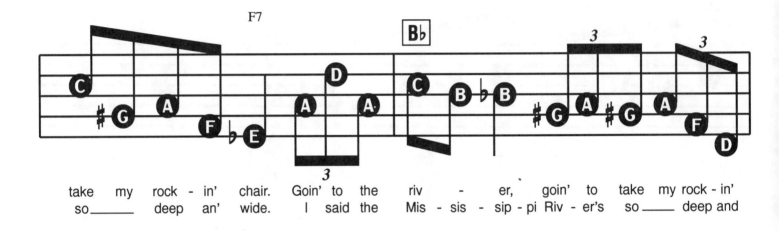

take my rock - in' chair. Goin' to the riv - er, goin' to take my rock - in'
so_____ deep an' wide. I said the Mis - sis - sip - pi Riv - er's so ___ deep and

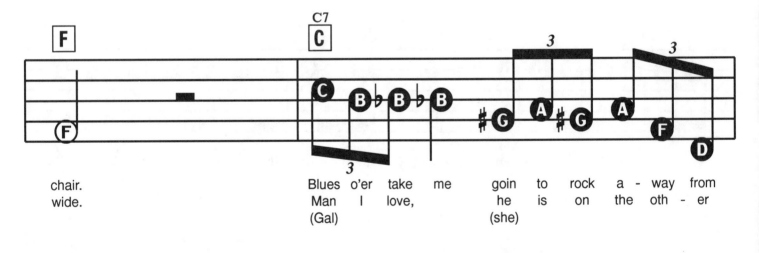

chair.   Blues o'er take me   goin to rock a - way from
wide.   Man I love,   he is on the oth - er
                (Gal)   (she)

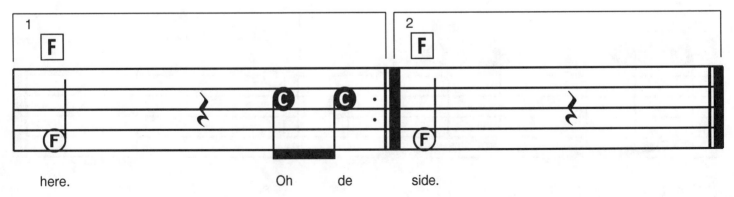

here.   Oh de side.

I Love A Piano

Registration 8
Rhythm: Swing

Words and Music by
Irving Berlin

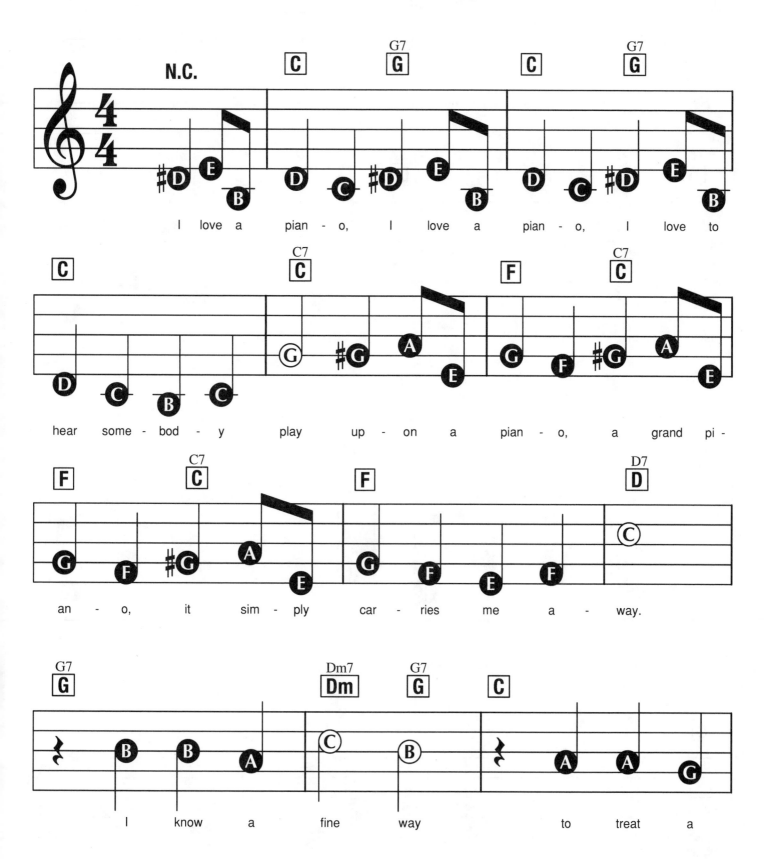

68

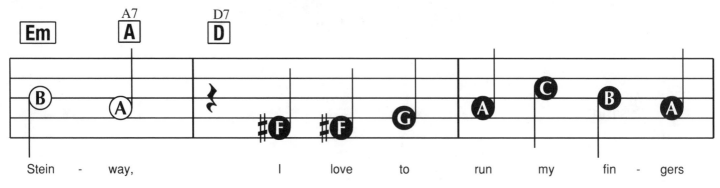

Stein - way,   I   love to   run my fin - gers

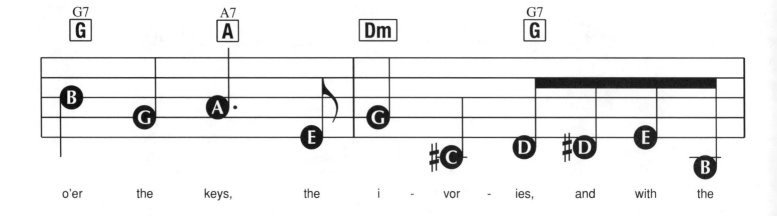

o'er   the   keys,   the   i - vor - ies,   and   with   the

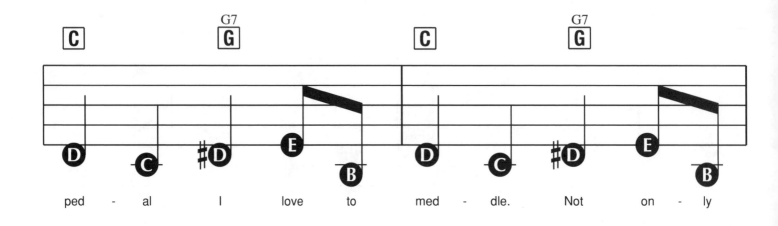

ped - al   I   love to   med - dle.   Not   on - ly

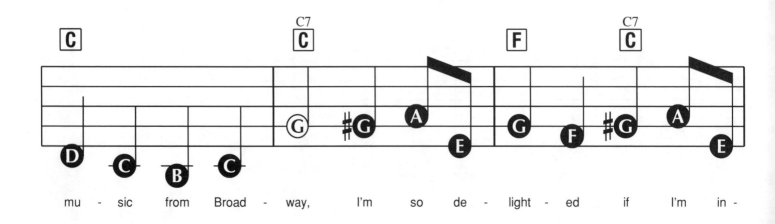

mu - sic from Broad - way, I'm so de - light - ed if I'm in-

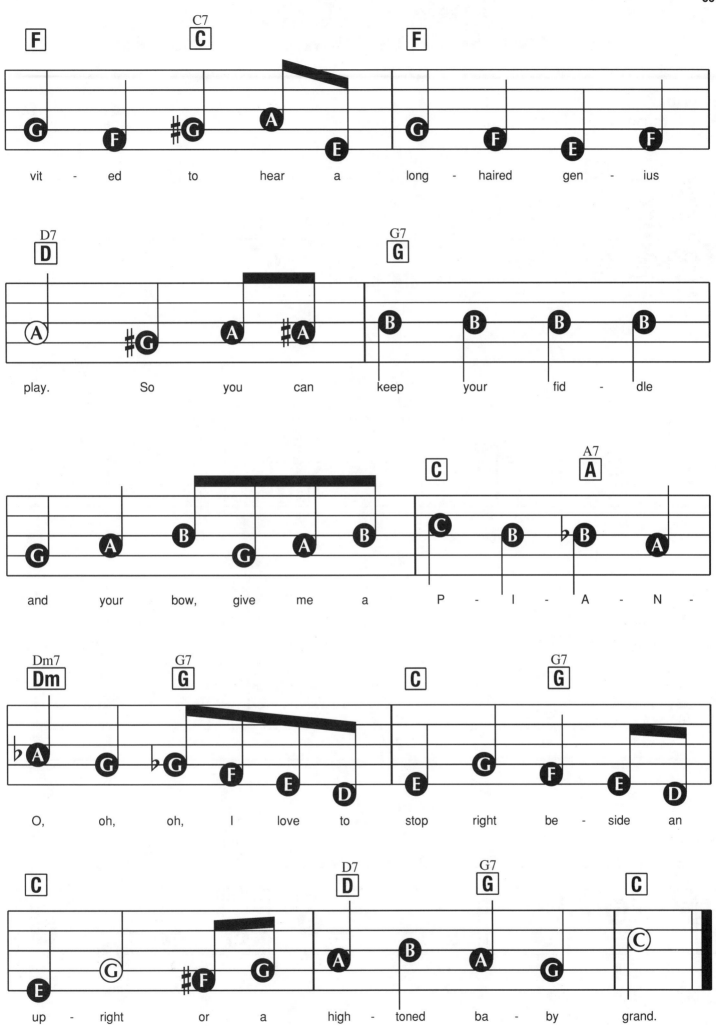

I Want A Girl
(Just Like The Girl That Married Dear Old Dad)

Registration 2
Rhythm: Swing or Jazz

By Will Dillon
and Harry Von Tilzer

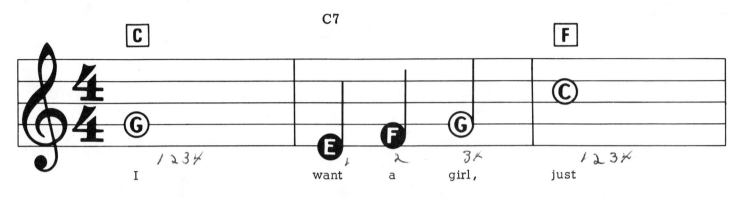

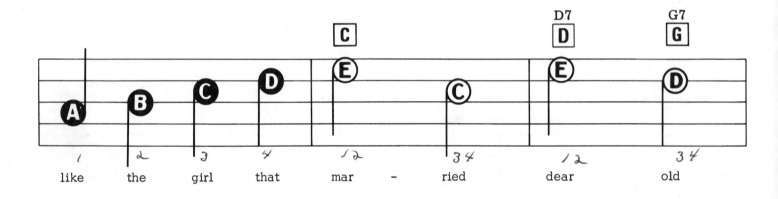

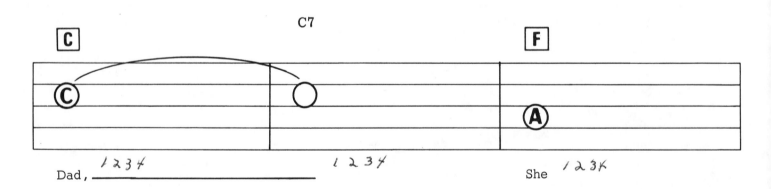

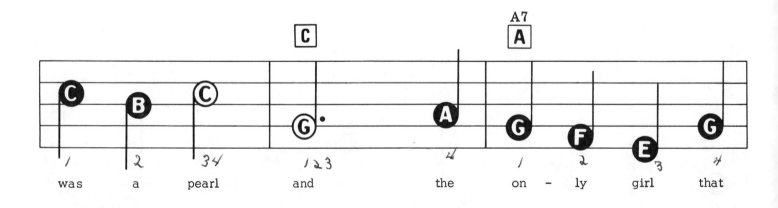

71

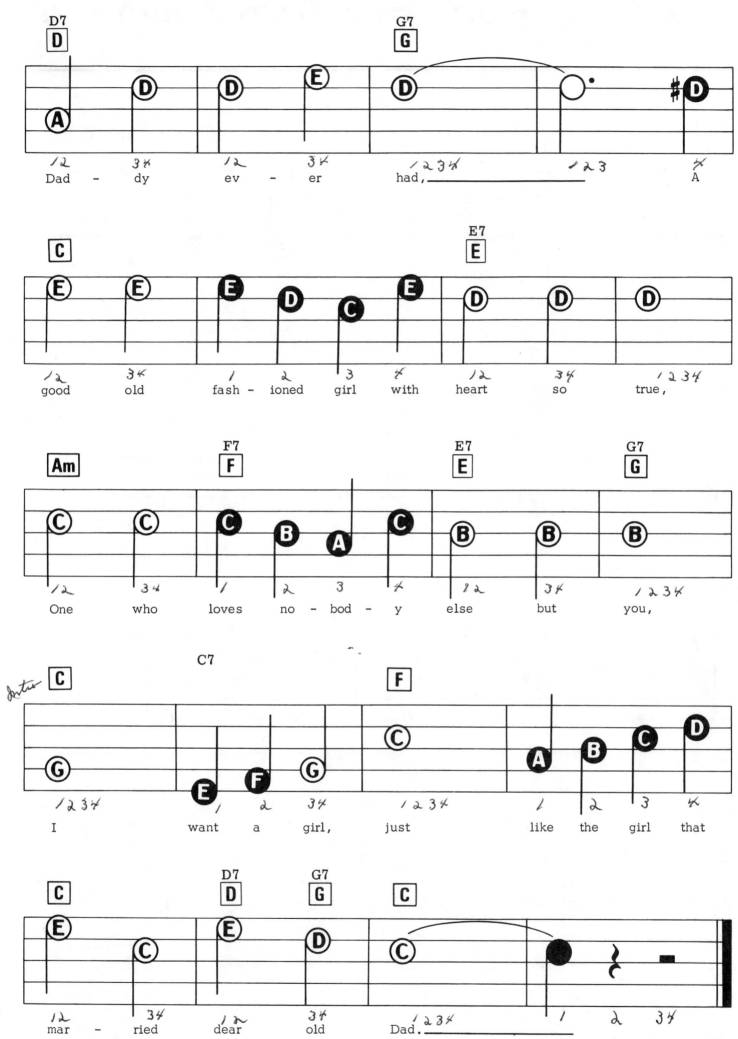

I'm Falling In Love With Someone

Registration 5
Rhythm: Waltz

Words by Rida Johnson Young
Music by Victor Herbert

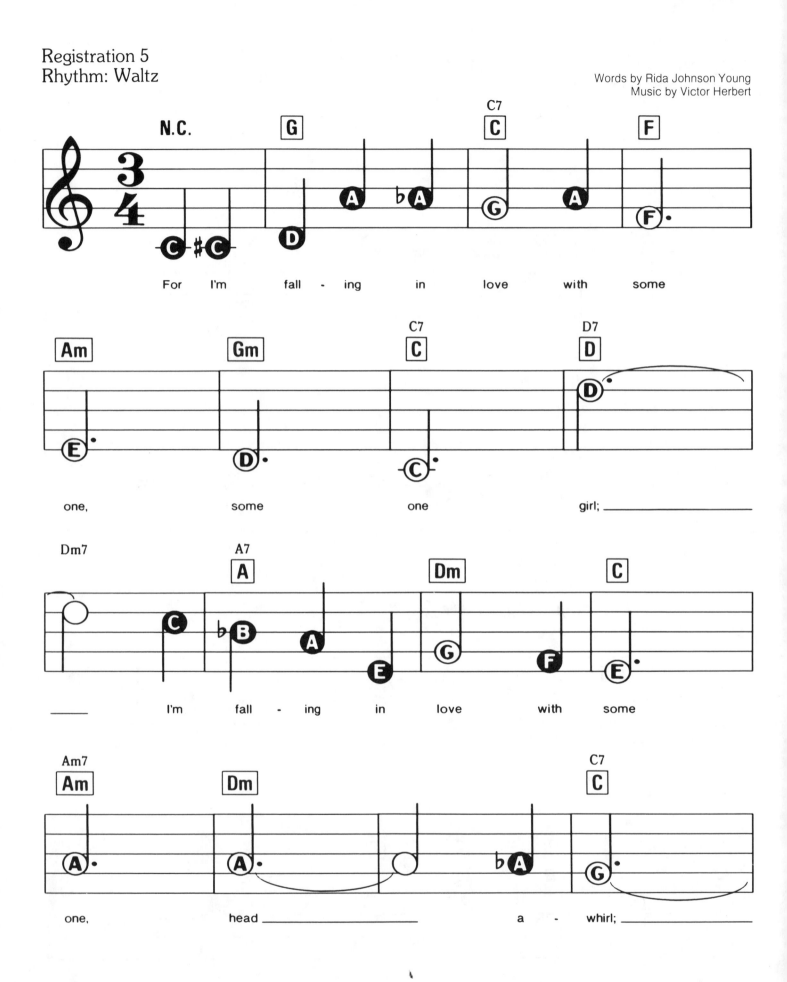

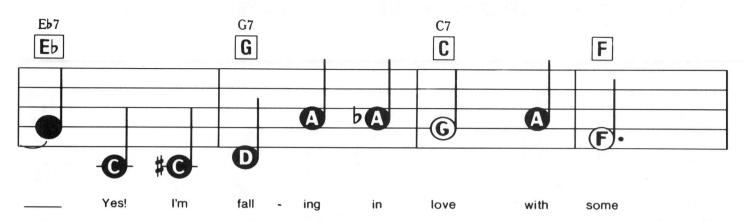

Yes! I'm fall - ing in love with some

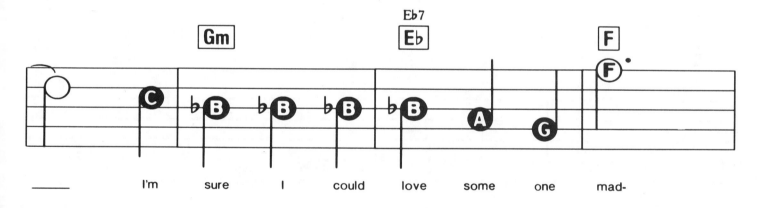

one, plain to see, _____

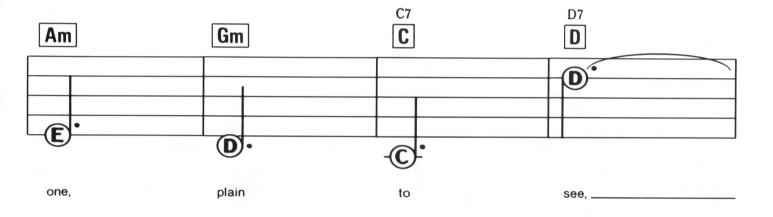

_____ I'm sure I could love some one mad-

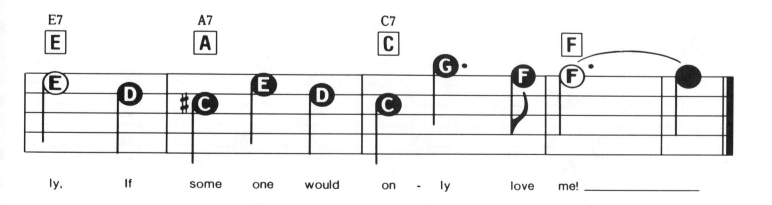

ly, If some one would on - ly love me! _____

If I Had My Way

Registration 2
Rhythm: Waltz

Words by Lou Klein
Music by James Kendis

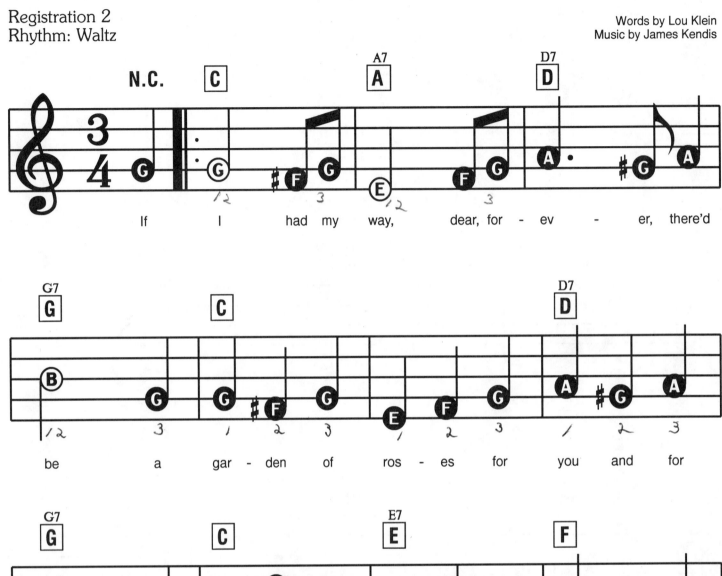

If I had my way, dear, for - ev - er, there'd

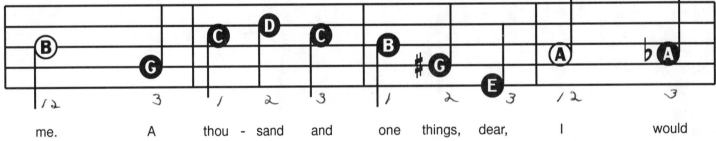

be a gar - den of ros - es for you and for

me. A thou - sand and one things, dear, I would

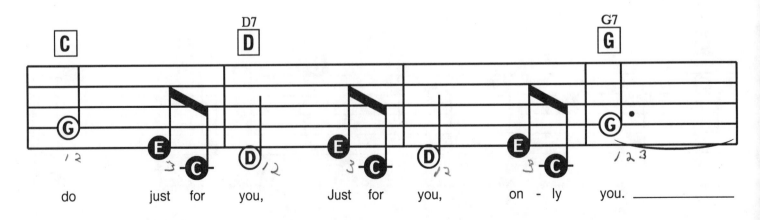

do just for you, Just for you, on - ly you. _____

75

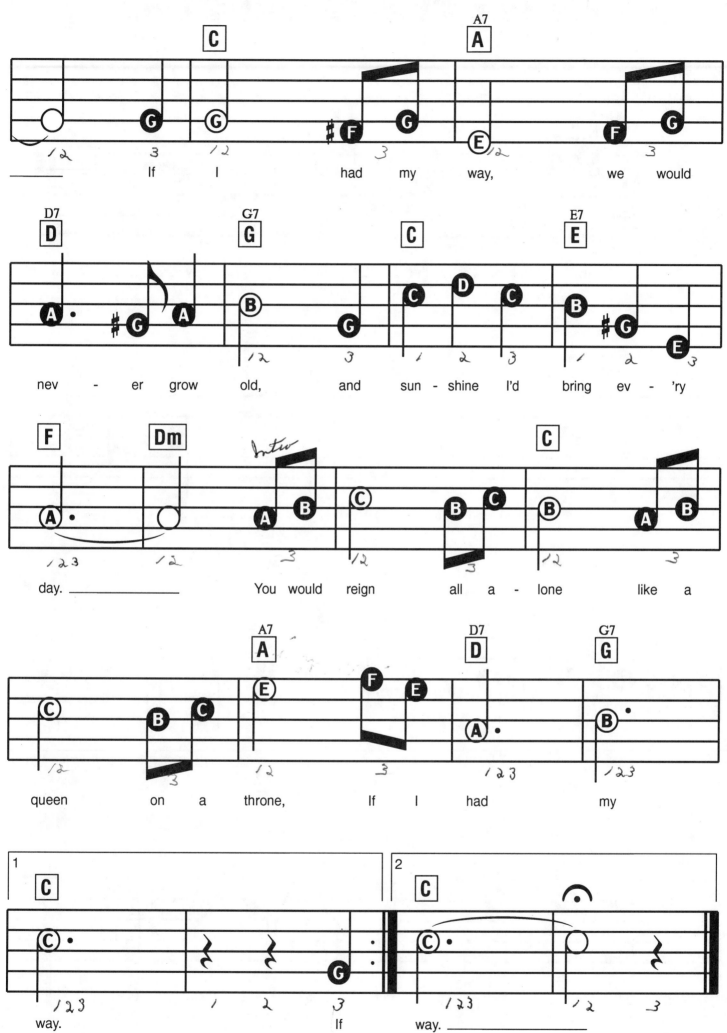

If I Knock The 'L' Out Of Kelly

Registration 8
Rhythm: Waltz

Words by Sam M. Lewis and Joe Young
Music by Bert Grant

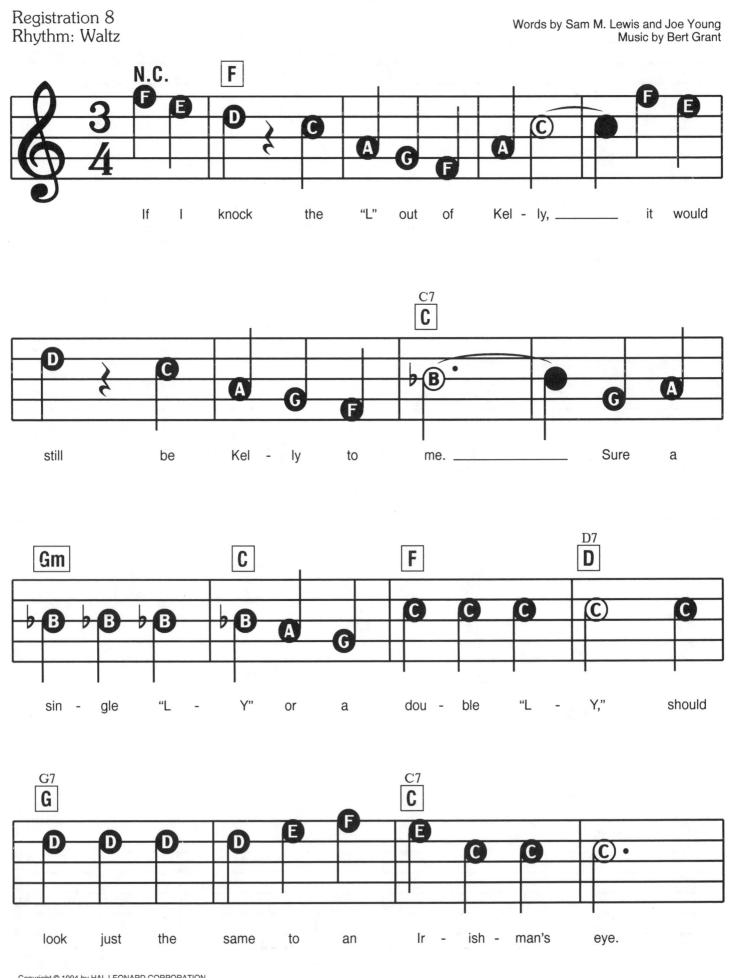

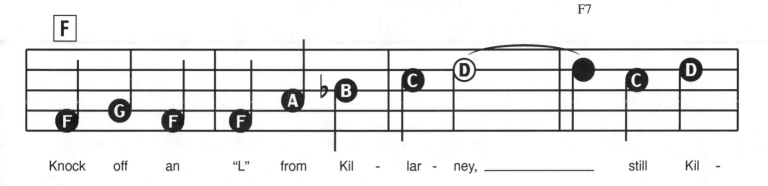

Knock off an "L" from Kil - lar - ney, _____ still Kil -

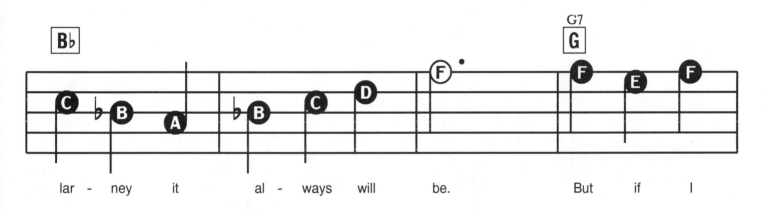

lar - ney it al - ways will be. But if I

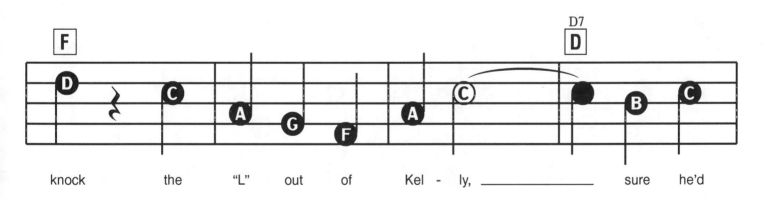

knock the "L" out of Kel - ly, _____ sure he'd

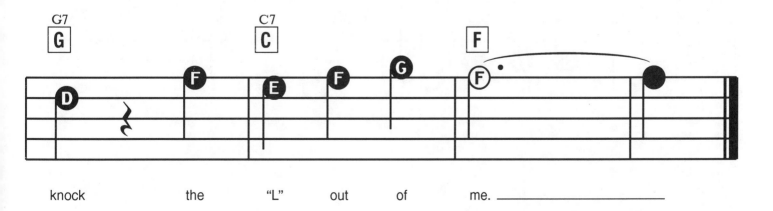

knock the "L" out of me. _____

Indiana
(Back Home Again In Indiana)

Registration 3
Rhythm: Swing

Words by Ballard MacDonald
Music by James F. Hanley

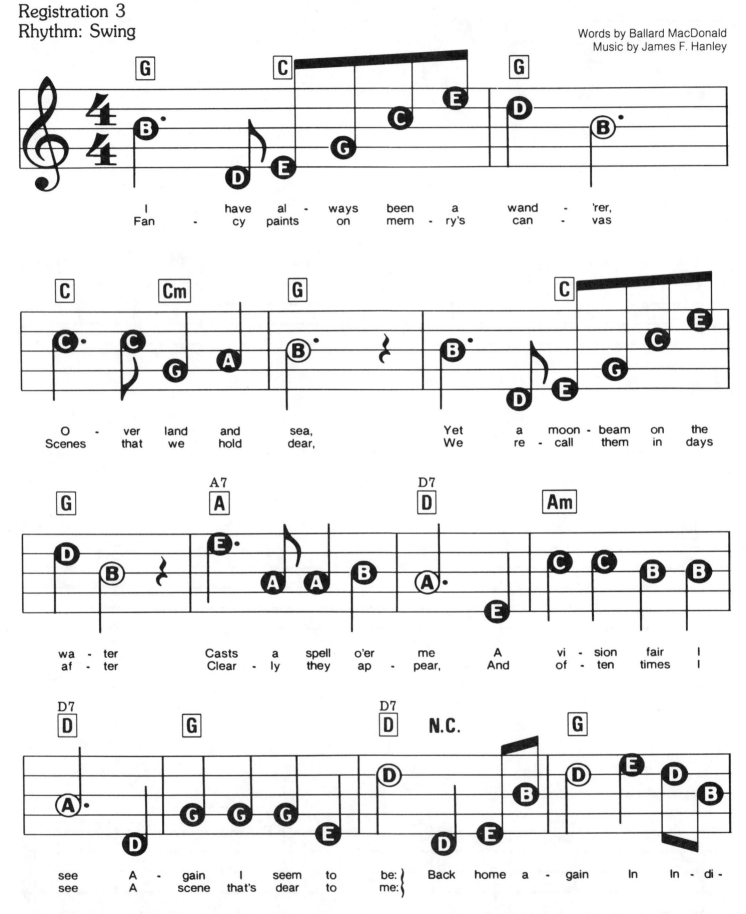

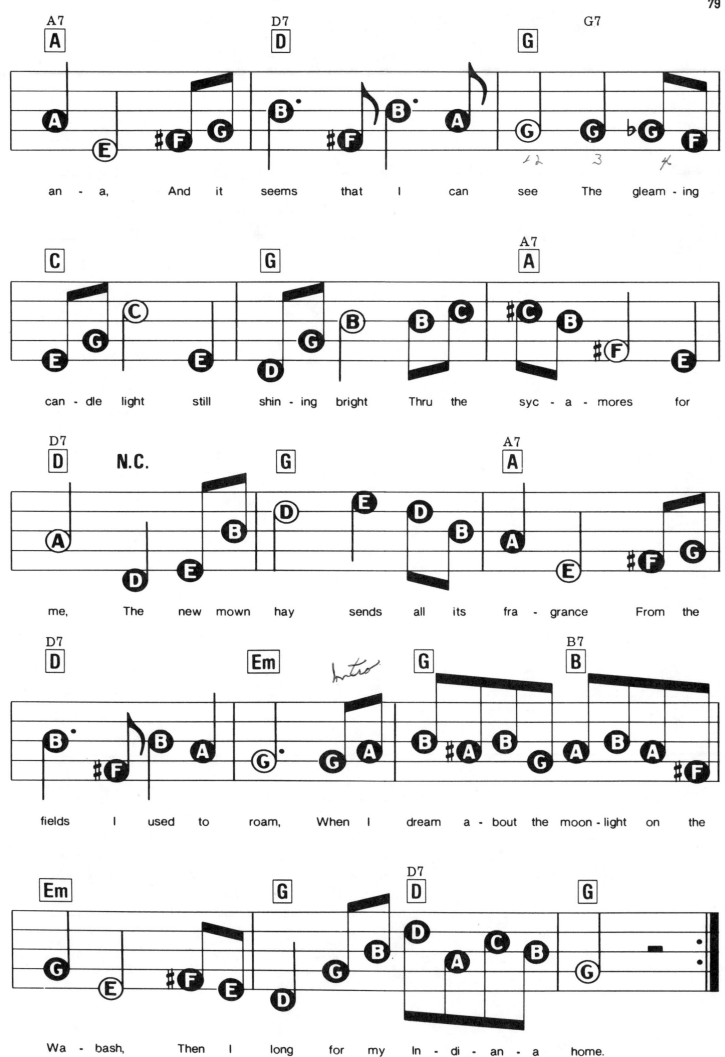

It's A Long, Long Way To Tipperary

Registration 8
Rhythm: March

Words and Music by Jack Judge
and Harry Williams

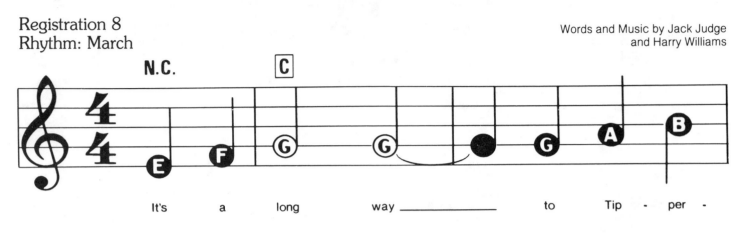

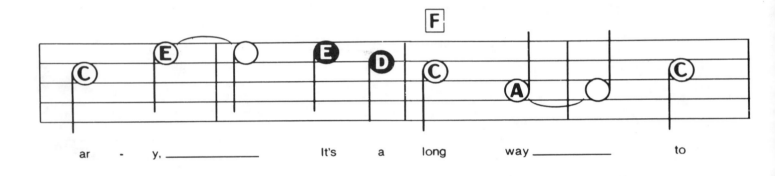

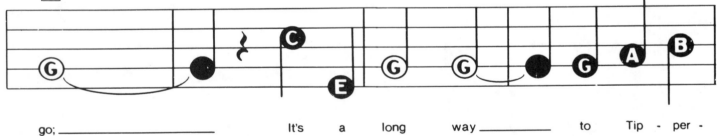

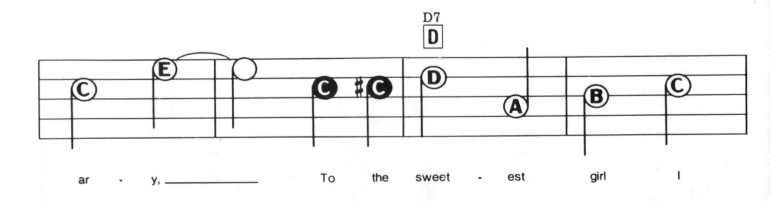

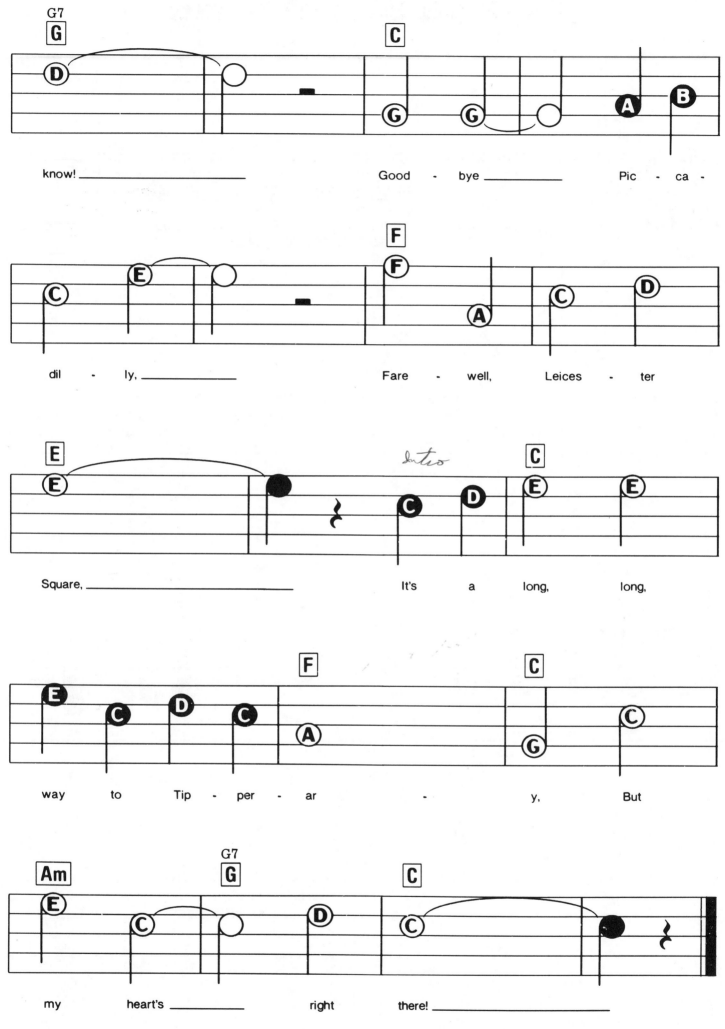

Italian Street Song

Registration 5
Rhythm: Polka or Fox-Trot

Lyrics by Rida Johnson Young
Music by Victor Herbert

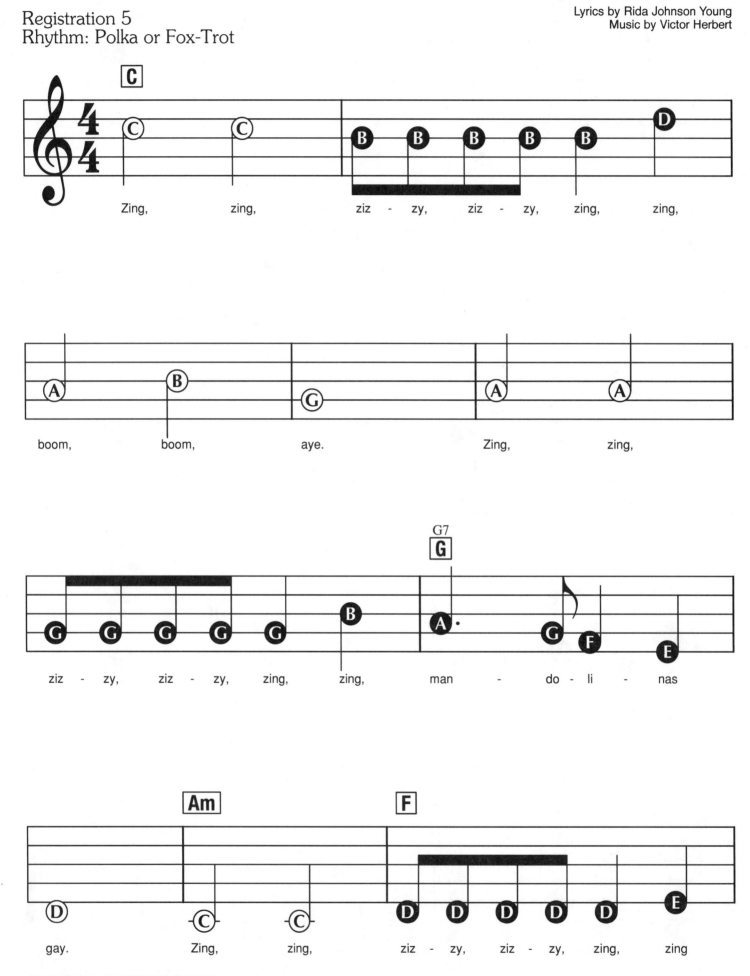

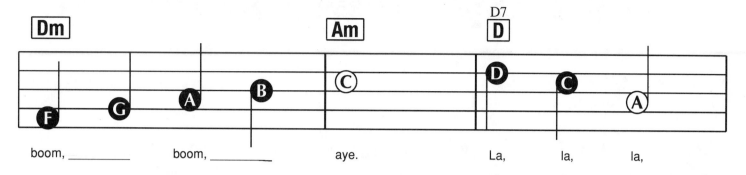

boom, _____ boom, _____ aye. La, la, la,

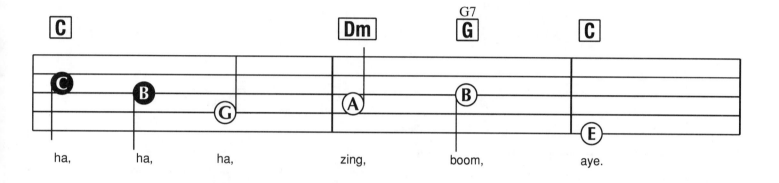

ha, ha, ha, zing, boom, aye.

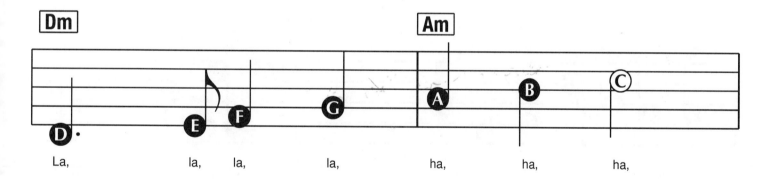

La, la, la, la, ha, ha, ha,

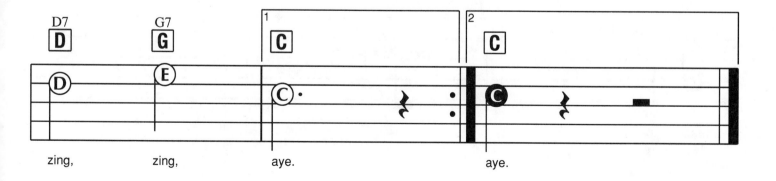

zing, zing, aye. aye.

Just A Baby's Prayer At Twilight

Registration 3
Rhythm: Fox Trot

Words by Sam M. Lewis and Joe Young
Music by M.K. Jerome

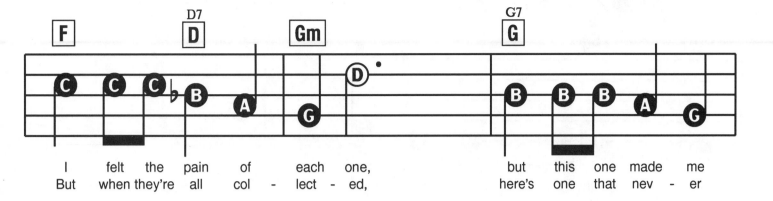

I felt the pain of each one, but this one made me
But when they're all col - lect - ed, here's one that nev - er

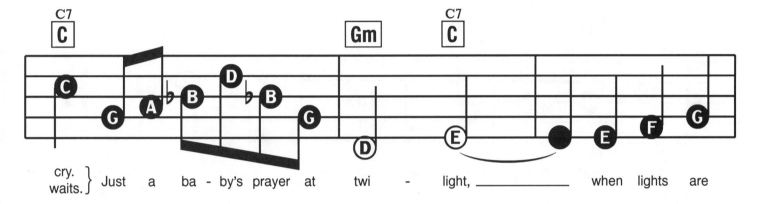

cry.
waits. } Just a ba - by's prayer at twi - light, _____ when lights are

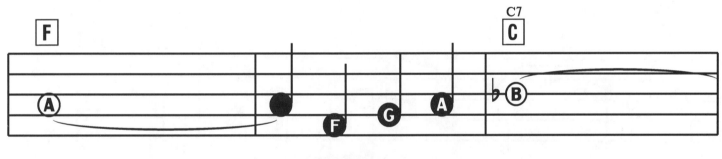

low. _____ Poor ba - by's years _____

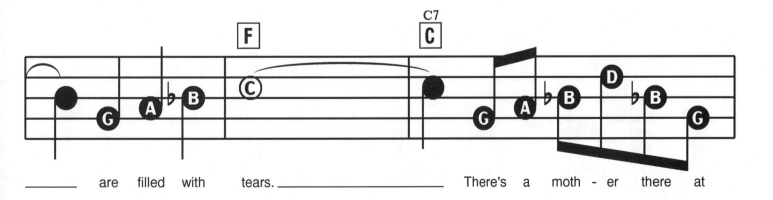

_____ are filled with tears. _____ There's a moth - er there at

86

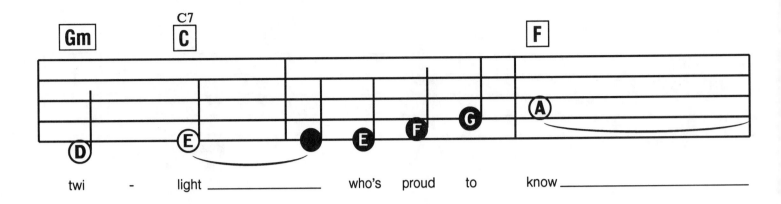

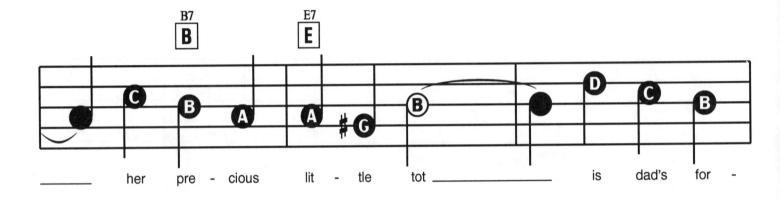

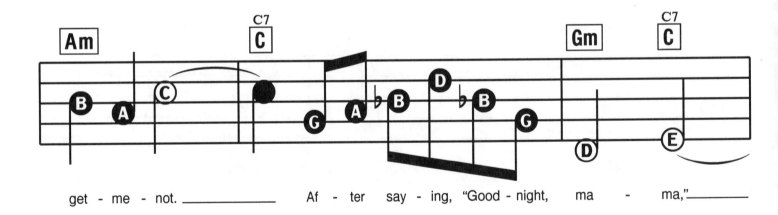

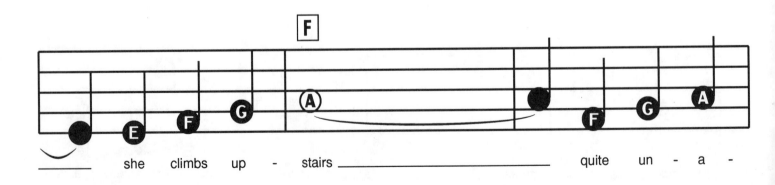

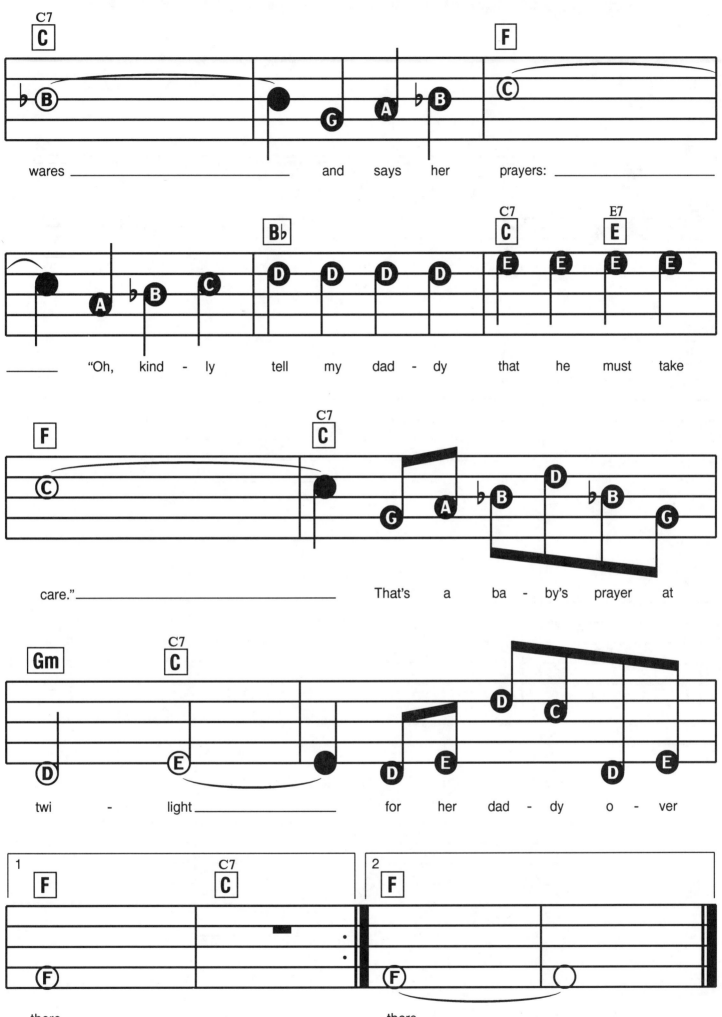

wares _____ and says her prayers: _____ "Oh, kind - ly tell my dad - dy that he must take care." _____ That's a ba - by's prayer at twi - light _____ for her dad - dy o - ver there.

there. _____

Let Me Call You Sweetheart

Words by Beth Slater Whitson
Music by Leo Friedman

Registration 3
Rhythm: Waltz

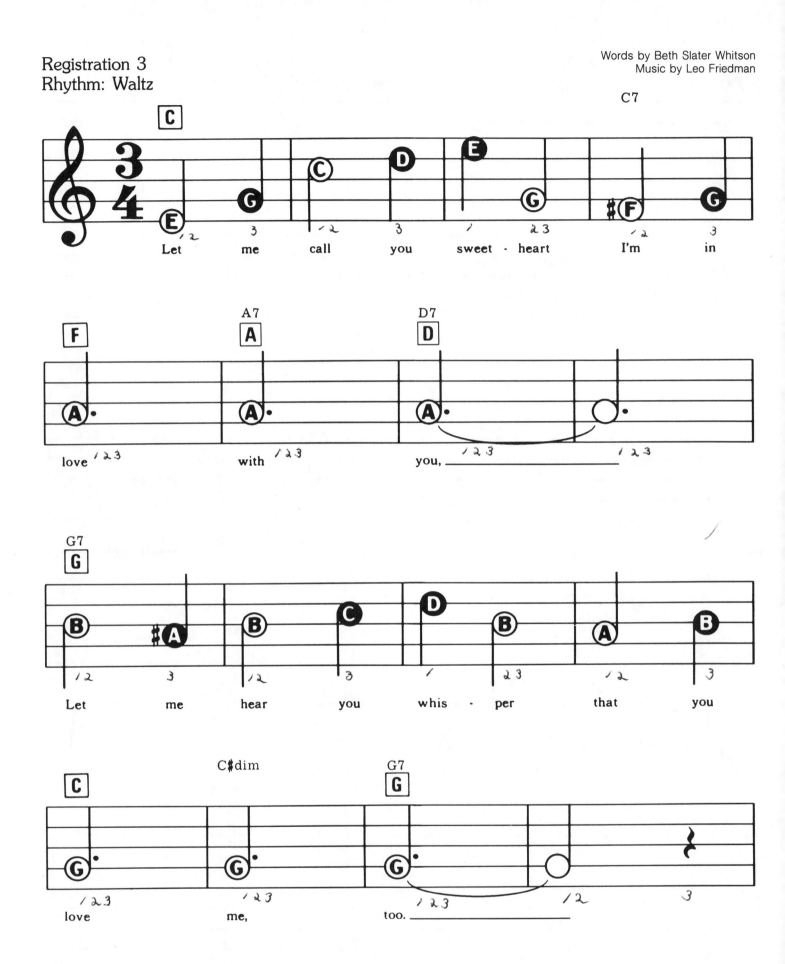

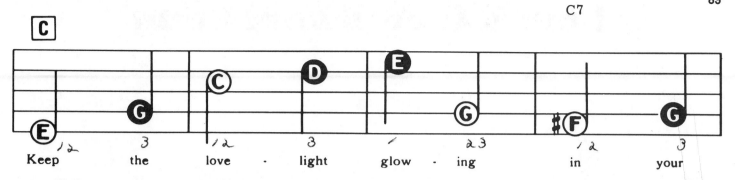

Keep the love - light glow - ing in your

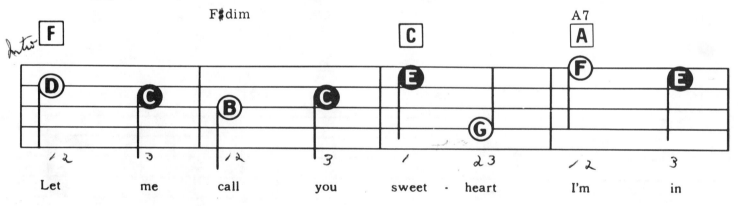

eyes so true. _____

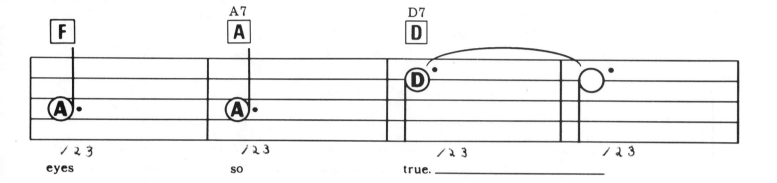

Let me call you sweet - heart I'm in

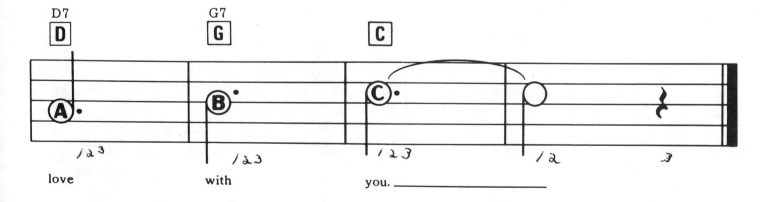

love with you. _____

Love's Own Sweet Song

Registration 3
Rhythm: Waltz

Lyrics by C.C.S. Cushing and E.P. Heath
Music by Emmerich Kalman

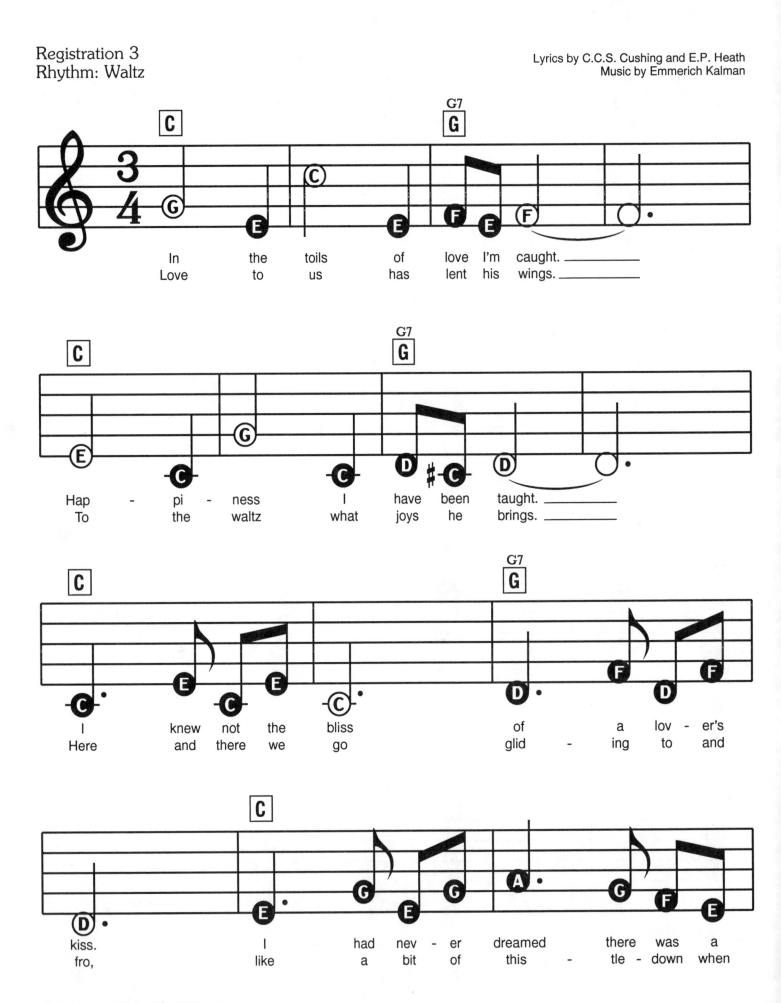

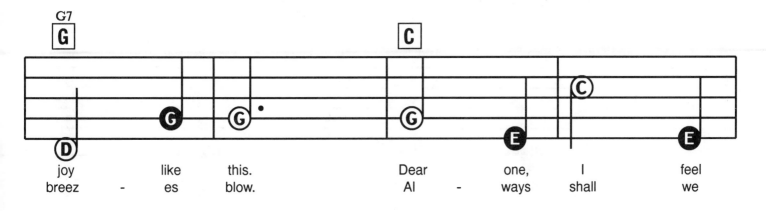

joy   like   this.   Dear   one,   I   feel
breez - es   blow.   Al - ways   shall   we

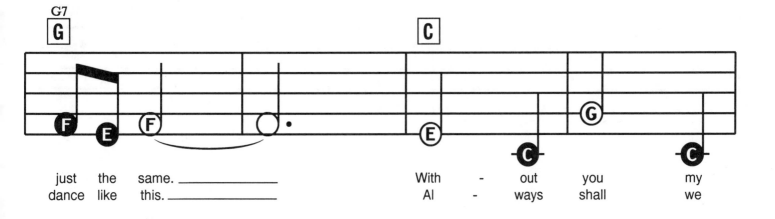

just   the   same. _____   With - out   you   my
dance like   this. _____   Al - ways   shall   we

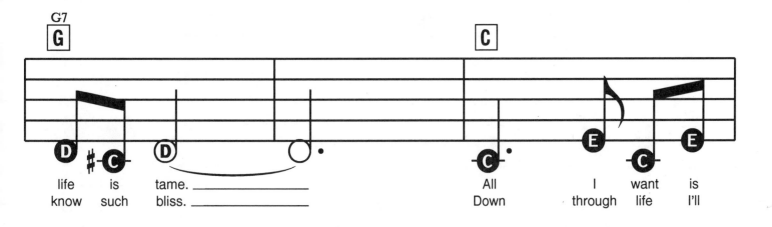

life   is   tame. _____   All   I   want   is
know such   bliss. _____   Down   through life   I'll

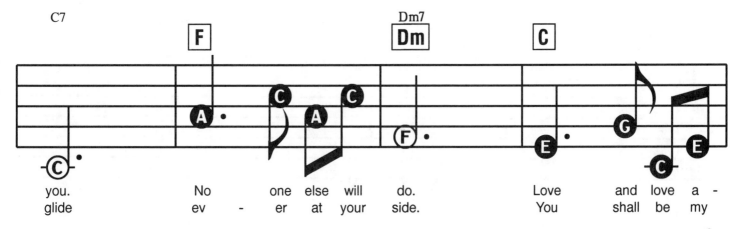

you.   No   one   else   will   do.   Love   and   love   a -
glide   ev - er   at   your side.   You   shall   be   my

over

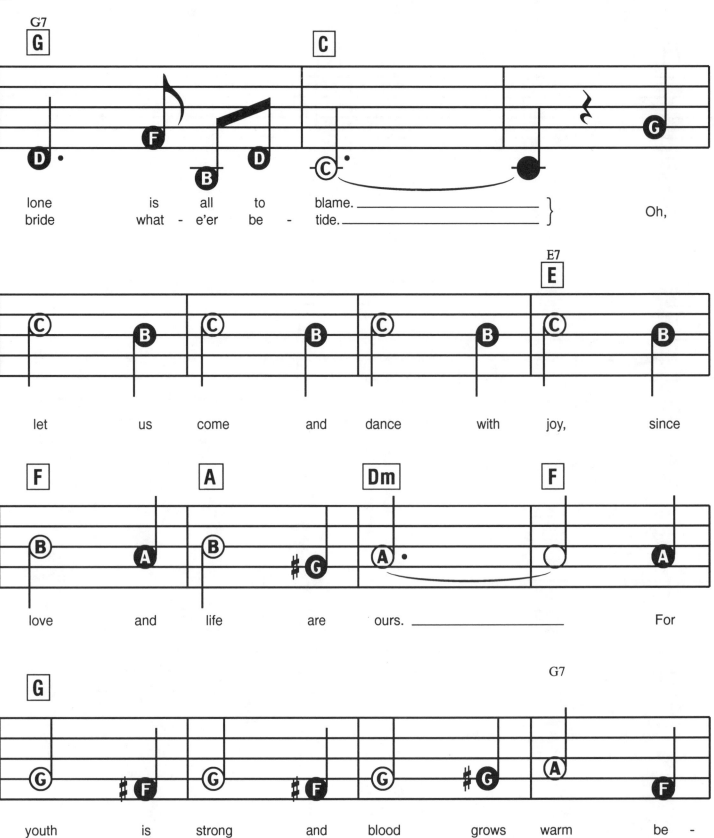

lone   is   all   to   blame. _____   Oh,

bride   what - e'er   be - tide. _____

let   us   come   and   dance   with   joy,   since

love   and   life   are   ours. _____   For

youth   is   strong   and   blood   grows   warm   be -

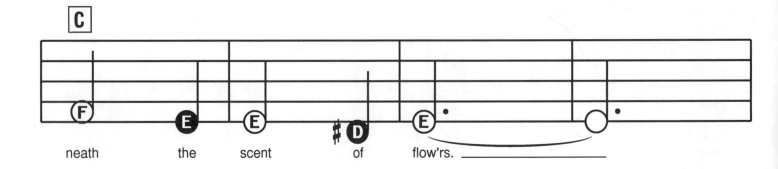

neath   the   scent   of   flow'rs. _____

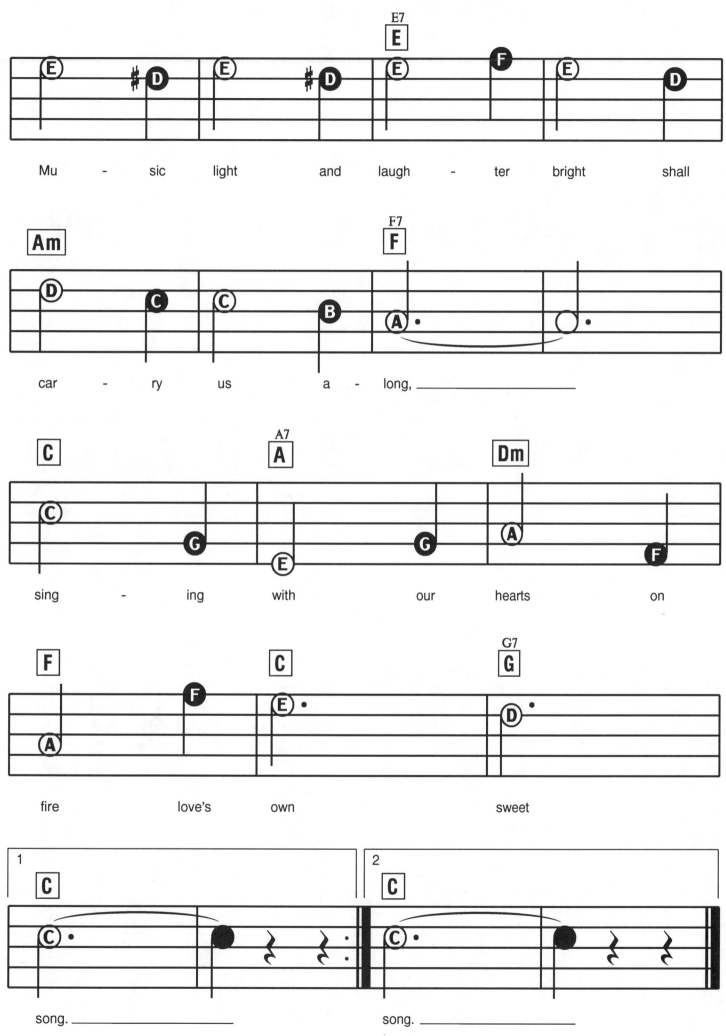

Moonlight Bay

Words by Edward Madden
Music by Percy Wenrich

Registration 2
Rhythm: Swing

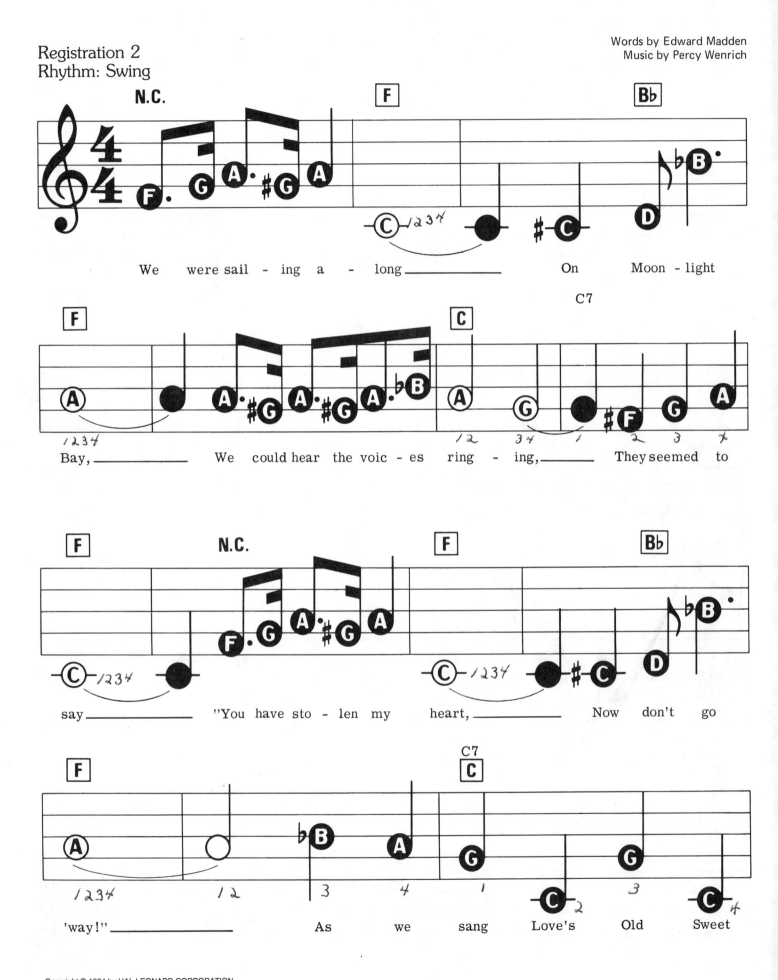

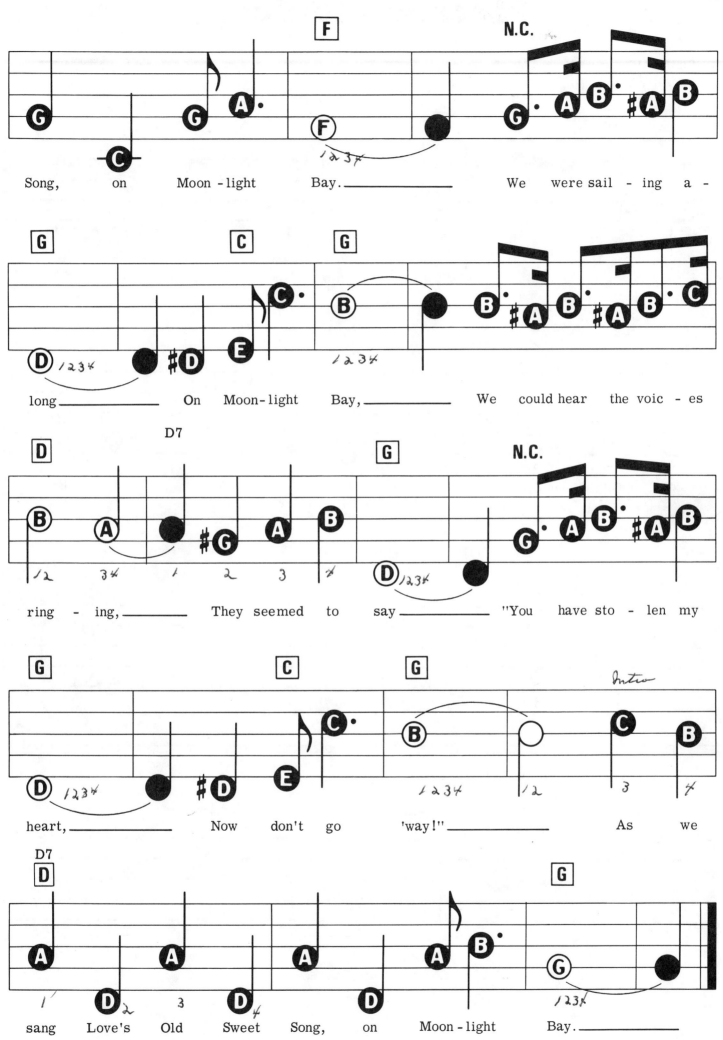

Mother Machree

Registration 2
Rhythm: Waltz

Words by Rida Johnson Young
Music by Ernest R. Ball and Chauncey Olcott

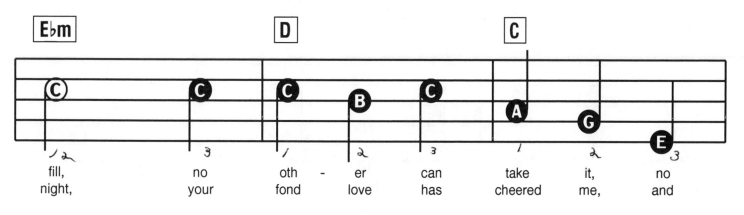

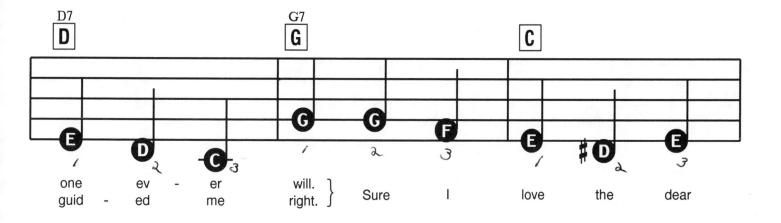

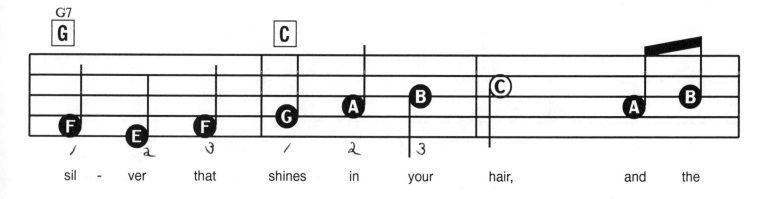

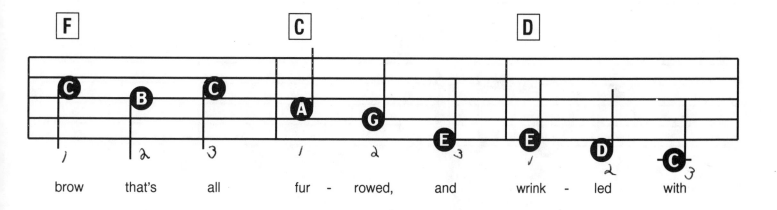

98

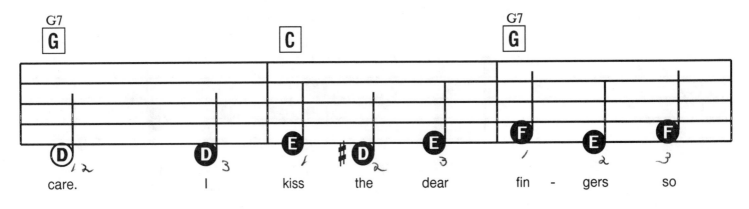

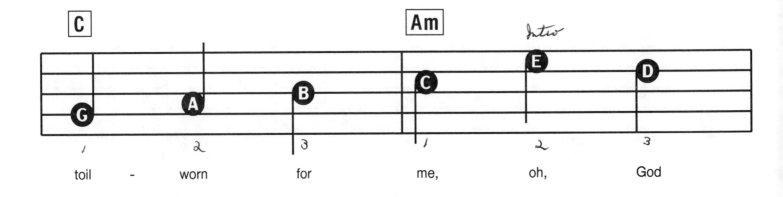

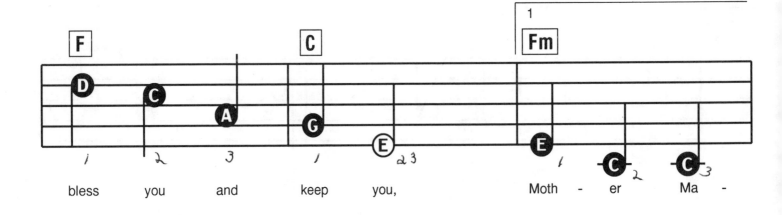

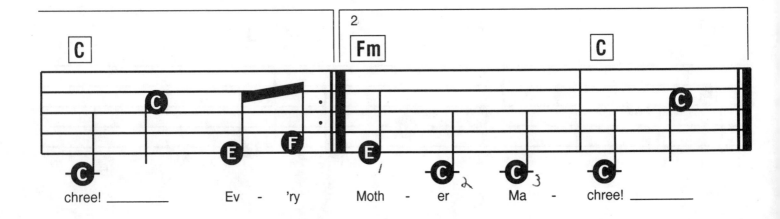

My Melancholy Baby

Registration 3
Rhythm: Swing

Words by George A. Norton
Music by Ernie Burnett

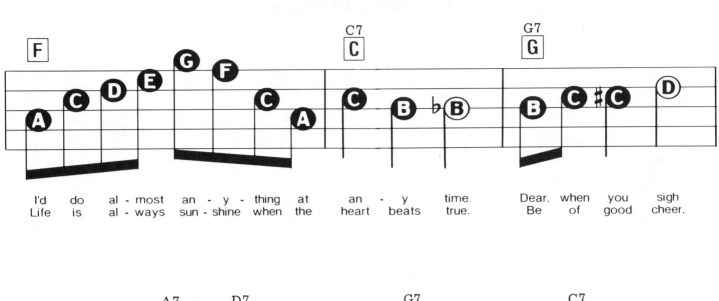

I'd   do   al - most   an - y - thing   at   an - y   time.   Dear,   when   you   sigh
Life   is   al - ways   sun - shine   when   the   heart   beats   true.   Be   of   good   cheer,

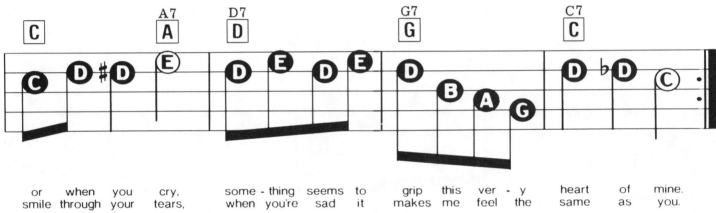

or   when   you   cry,   some - thing   seems   to   grip   this   ver - y   heart   of   mine.
smile   through   your   tears,   when   you're   sad   it   makes   me   feel   the   same   as   you.

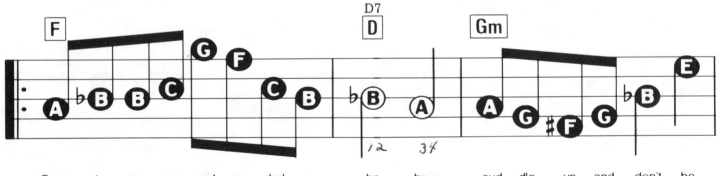

Come   to   me,   my   mel - an - chol - y   ba - by,   cud - dle   up   and   don't   be

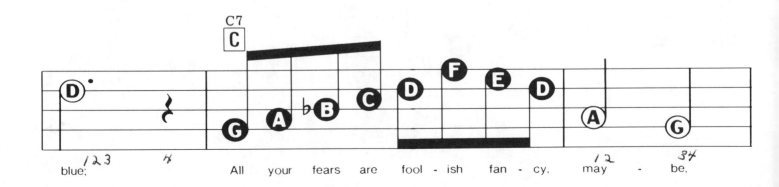

blue;   All   your   fears   are   fool - ish   fan - cy,   may - be,

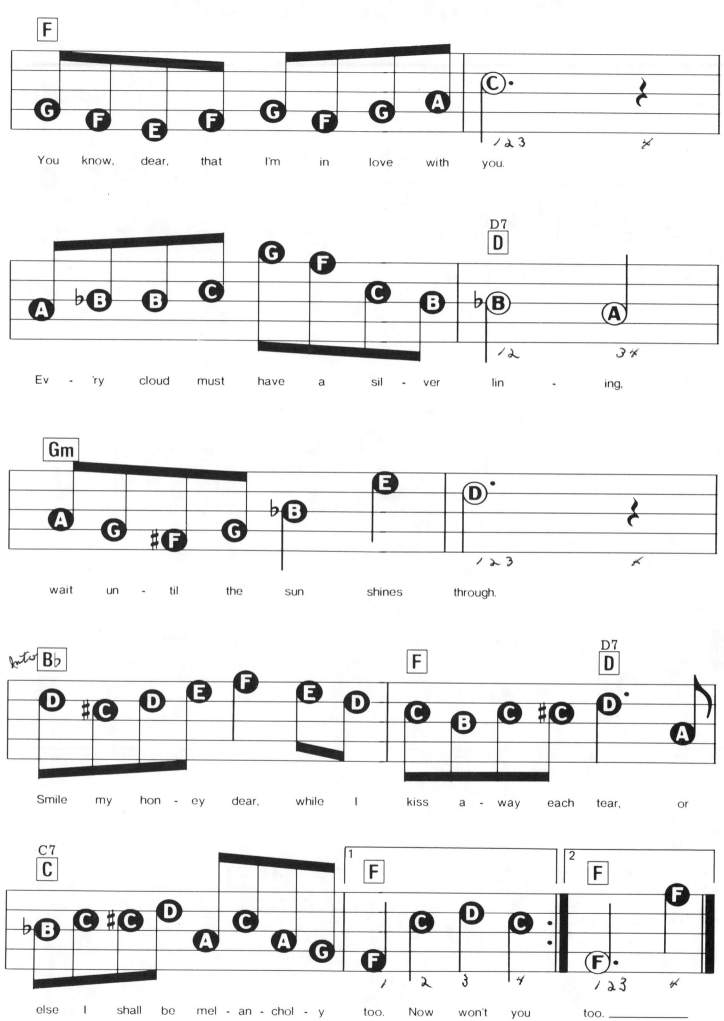

My Mother's Rosary

Registration 3
Rhythm: Fox-Trot

Music by George W. Meyer
Words by Sam M. Lewis

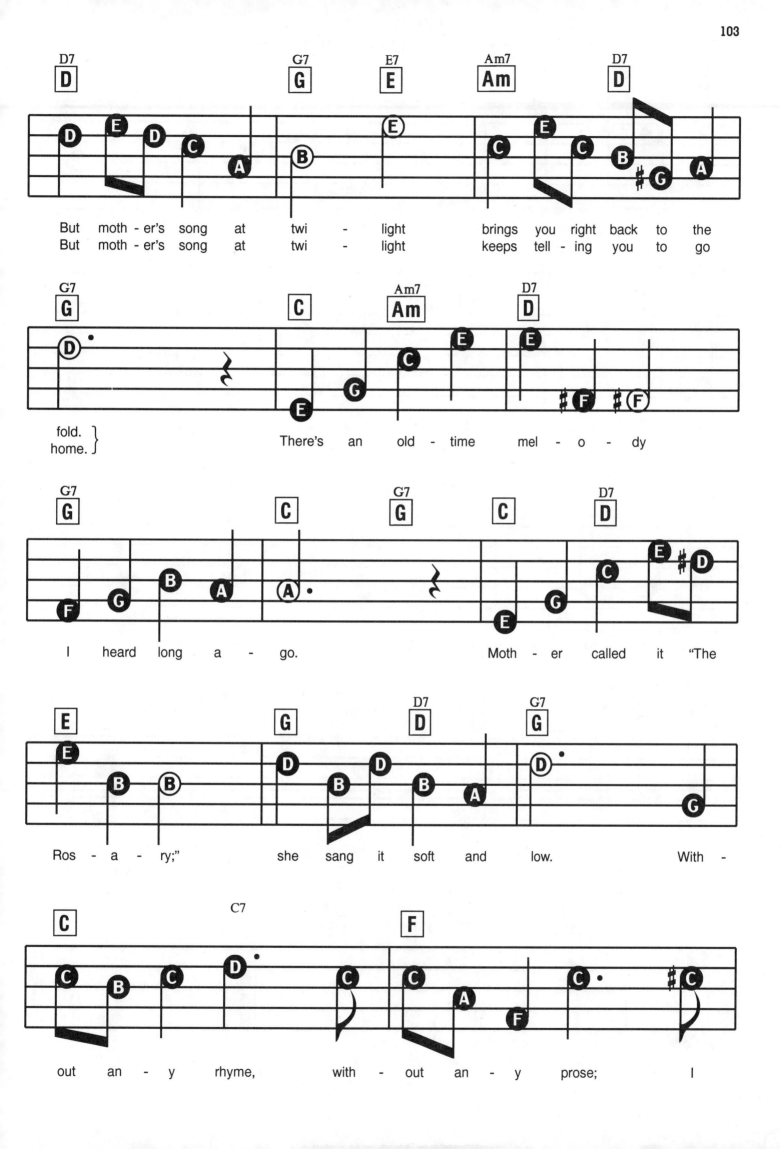

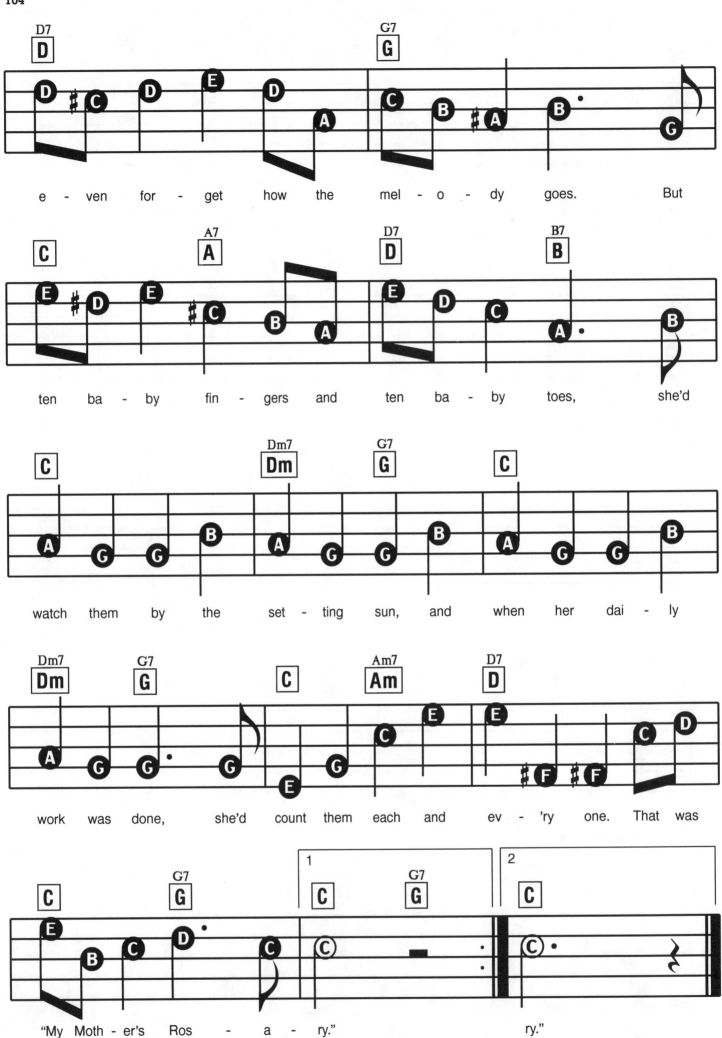

Rock-A-Bye Your Baby With A Dixie Melody

Registration 9
Rhythm: Fox-Trot or Swing

Words by Sam M. Lewis and Joe Young
Music by Jean Schwartz

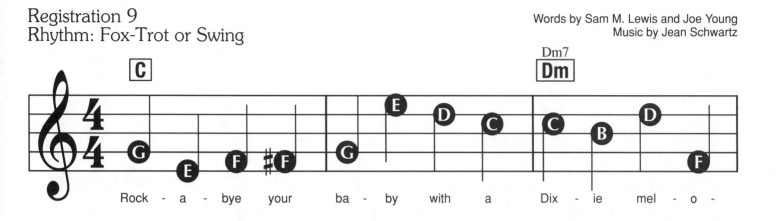

Rock - a - bye your ba - by with a Dix - ie mel - o -

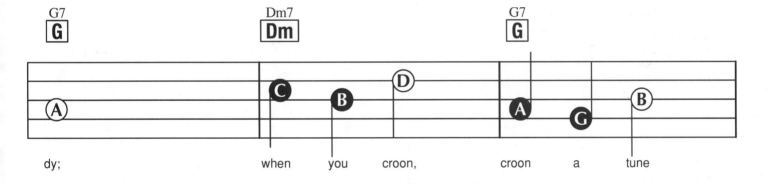

dy;   when you croon,   croon a tune

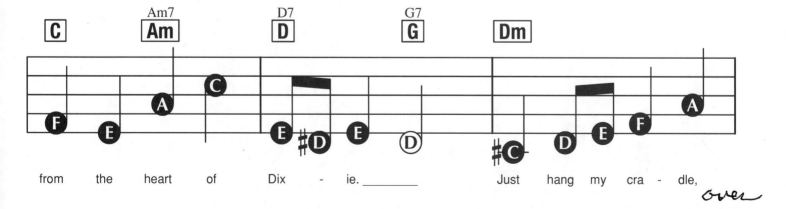

from the heart of Dix - ie. _____   Just hang my cra - dle,

over

106

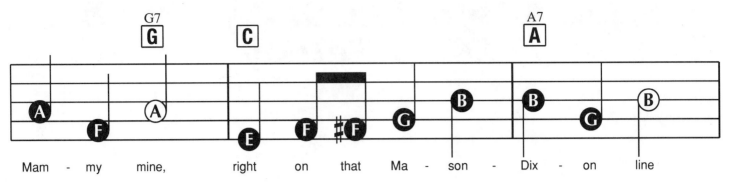

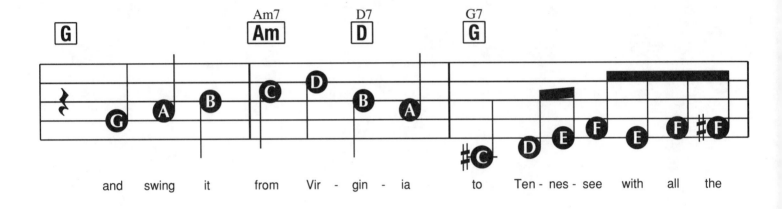

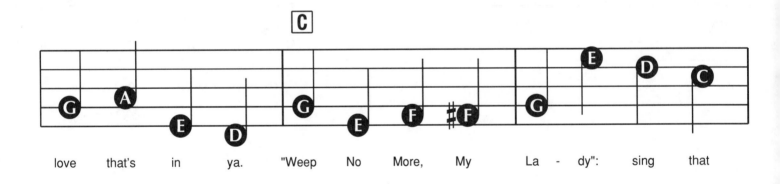

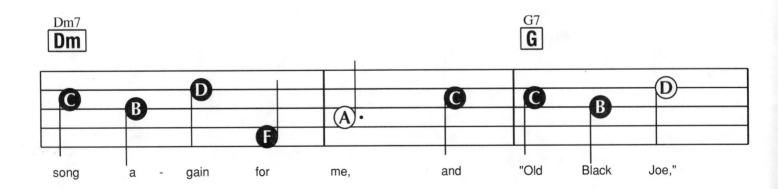

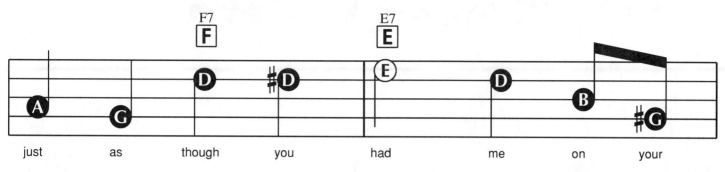

just   as   though   you   had   me   on   your

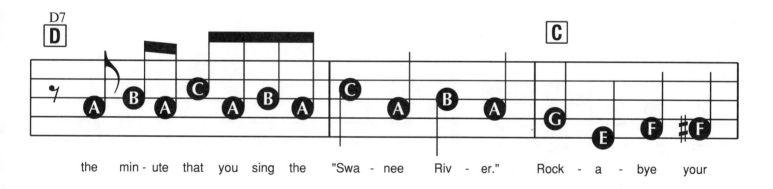

knee.   A   mil - lion   ba - by   kiss - es   I'll   de - liv - er

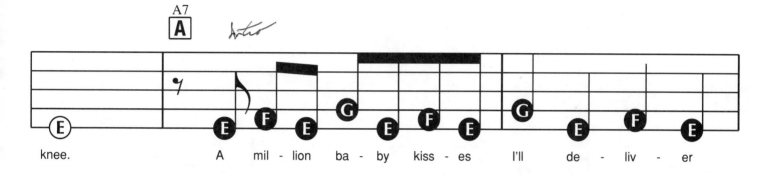

the   min - ute   that   you   sing   the   "Swa - nee   Riv - er."   Rock - a - bye   your

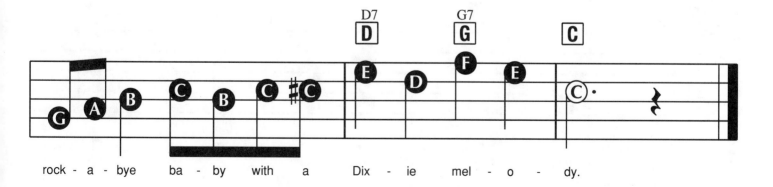

rock - a - bye   ba - by   with   a   Dix - ie   mel - o - dy.

Naughty Marietta

Registration 1
Rhythm: Waltz

Music by Victor Herbert
Words by Rida Johnson Young

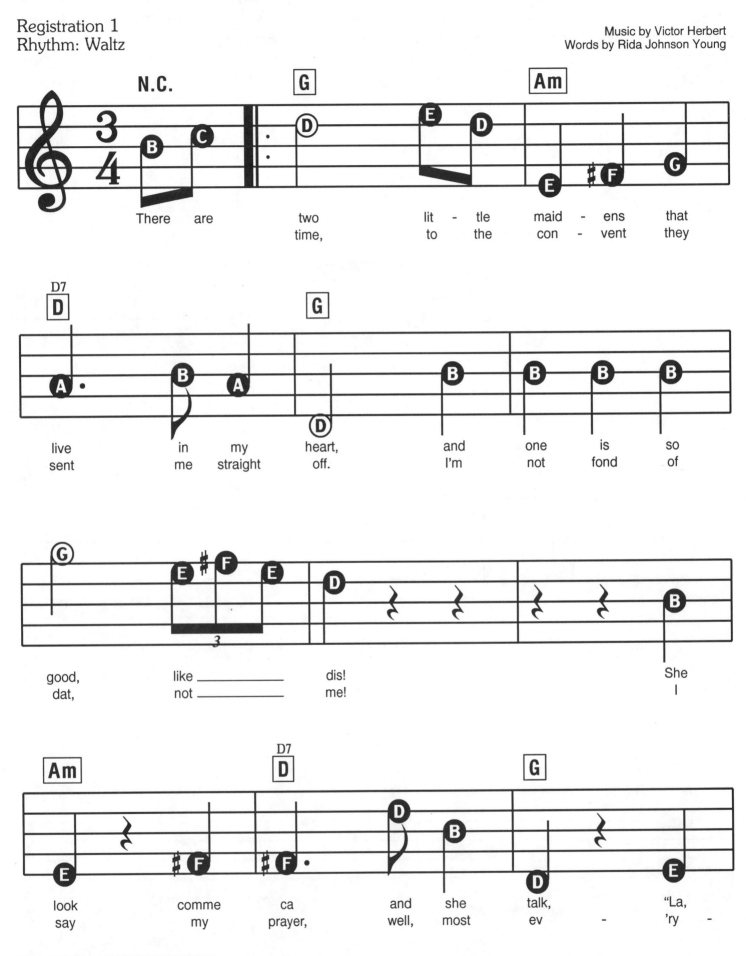

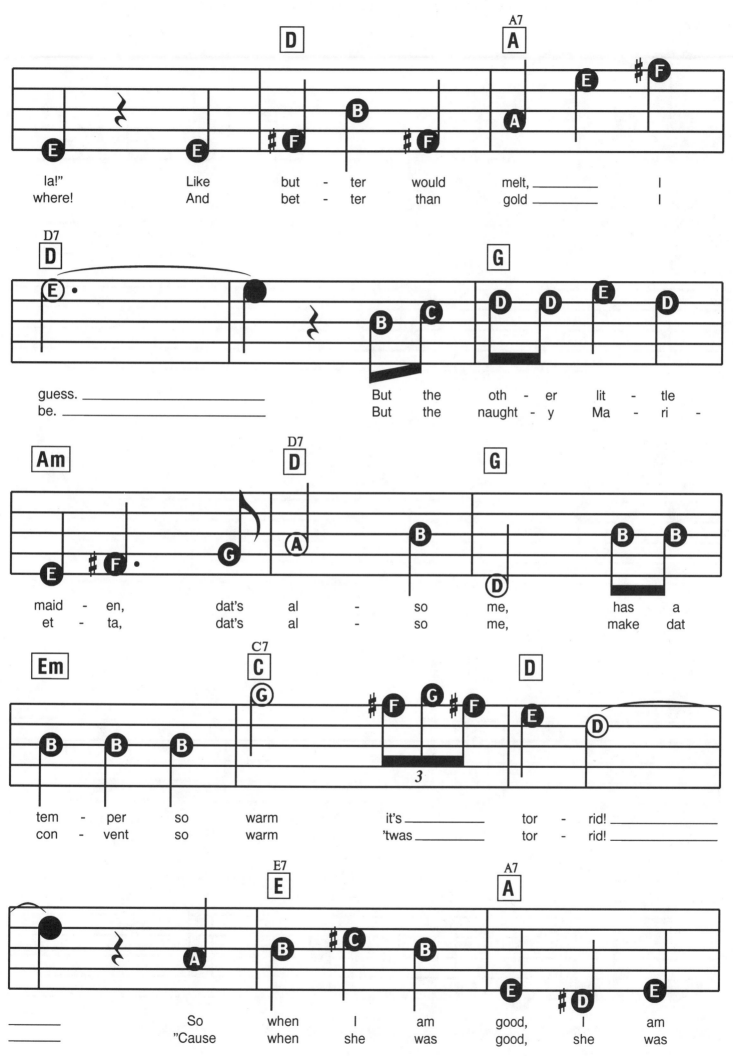

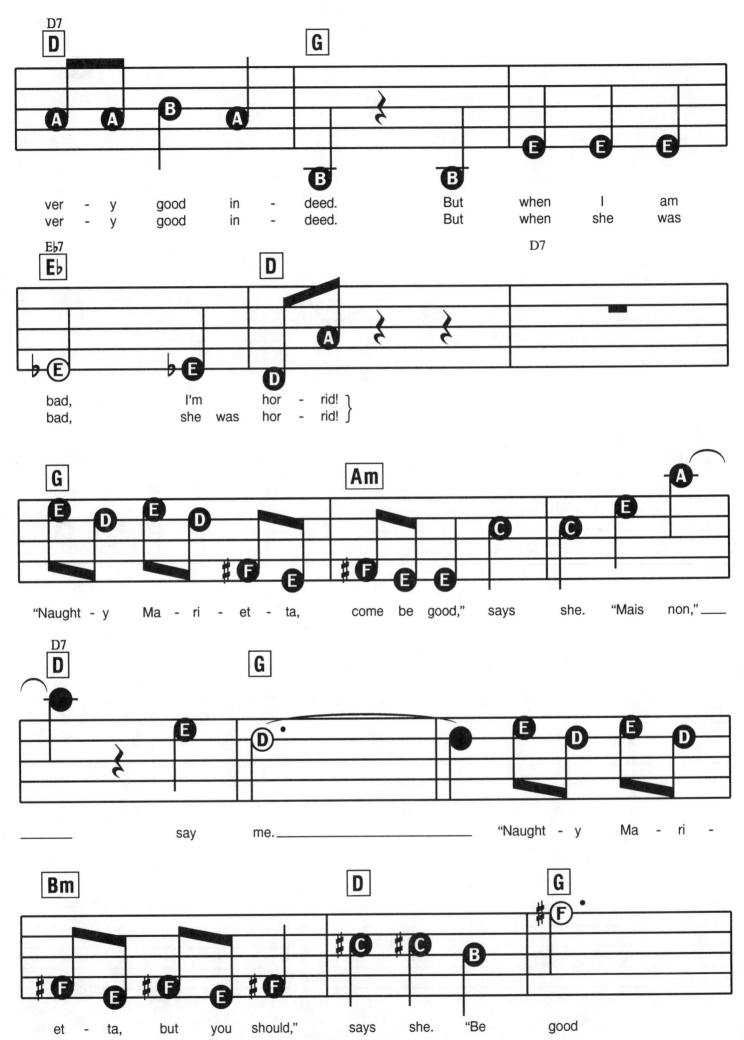

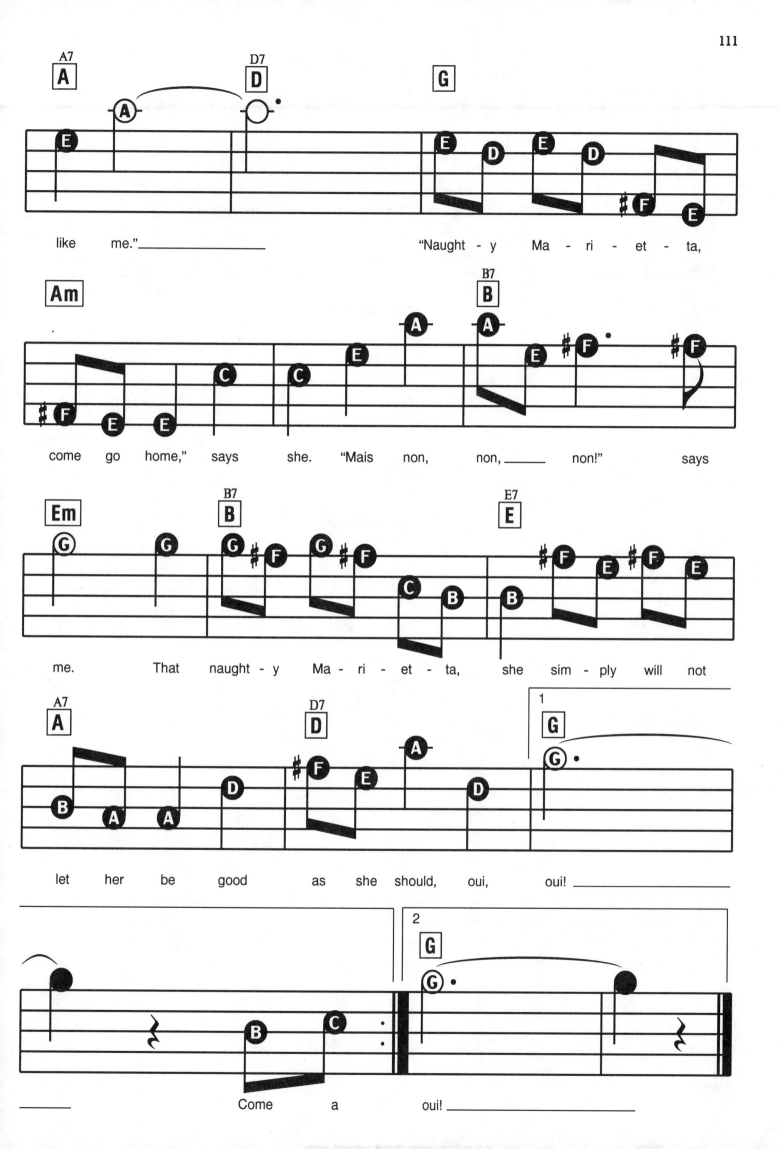

Oh! How I Hate
To Get Up In The Morning

Registration 2
Rhythm: 6/8 March

Words and Music by
Irving Berlin

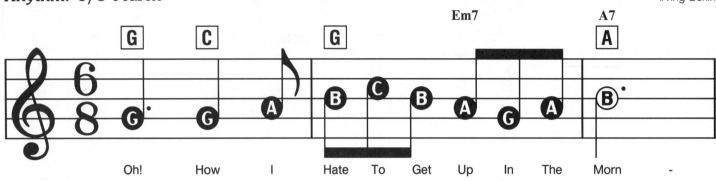

Oh! How I Hate To Get Up In The Morn -

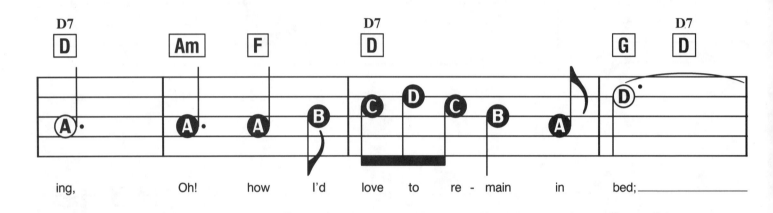

ing, Oh! how I'd love to re - main in bed;_____

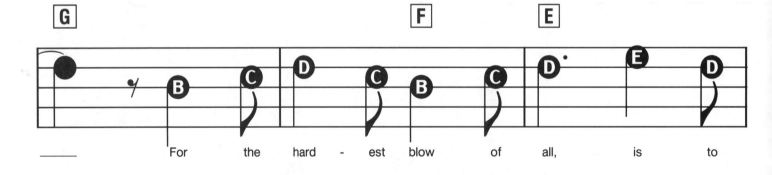

_____ For the hard - est blow of all, is to

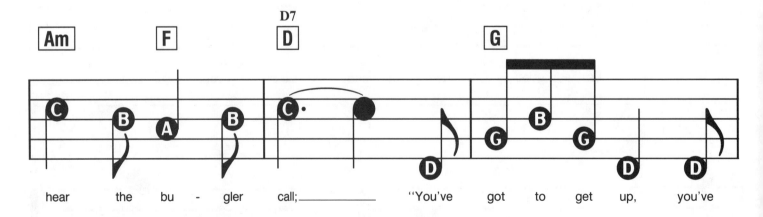

hear the bu - gler call;_____ "You've got to get up, you've

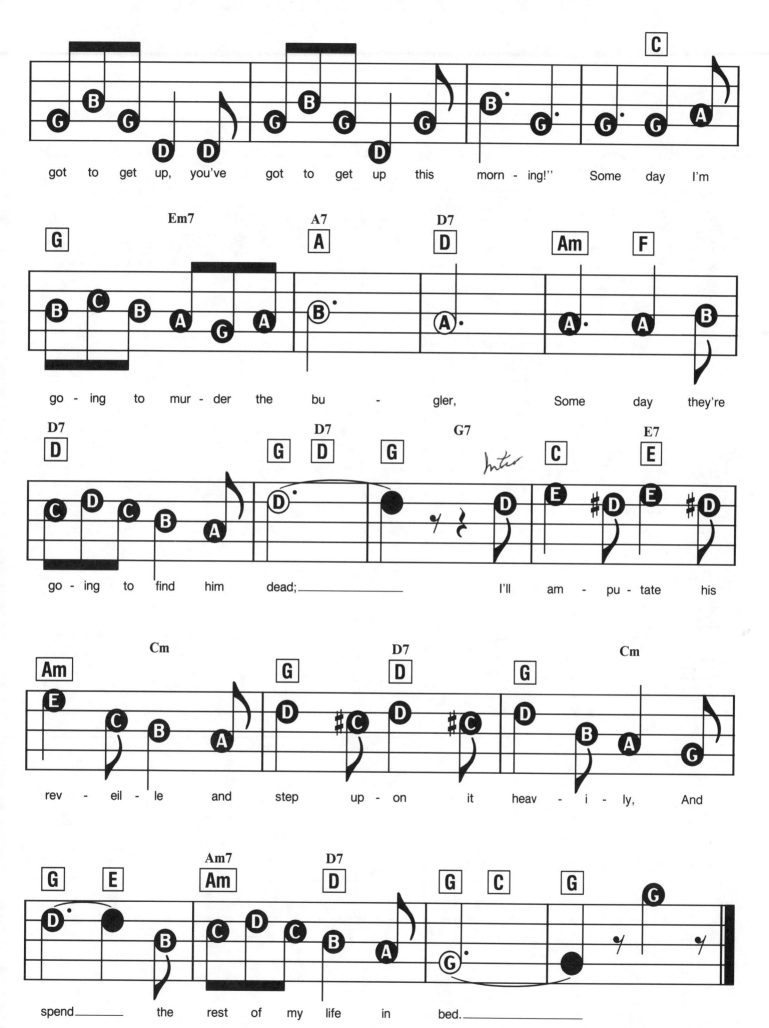

Oh, You Beautiful Doll

Registration 8
Rhythm: Fox Trot

Words by A. Seymour Brown
Music by Nat D. Ayer

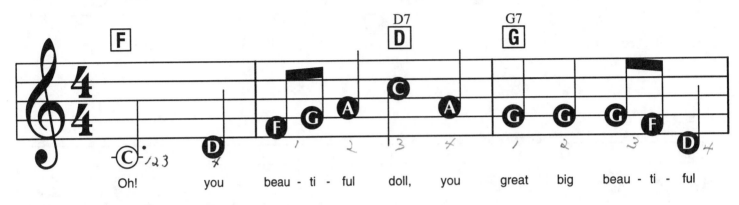

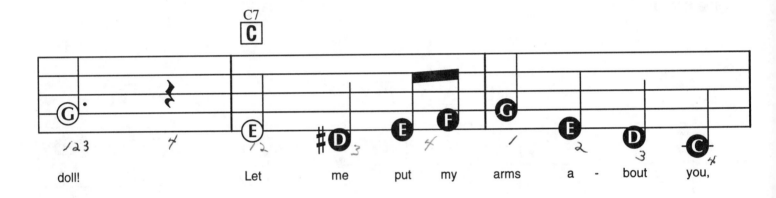

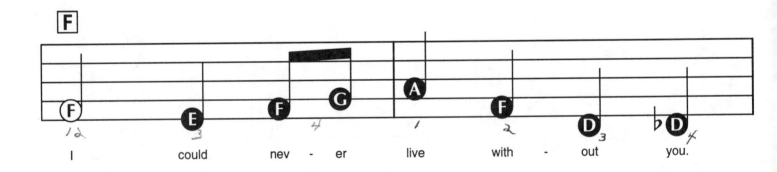

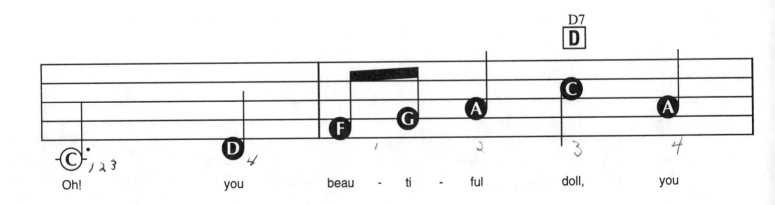

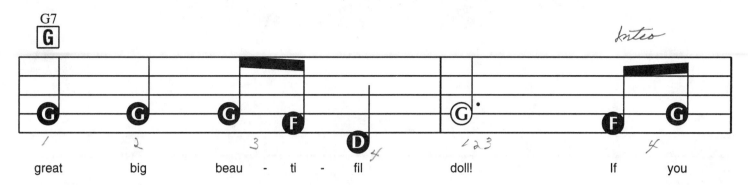

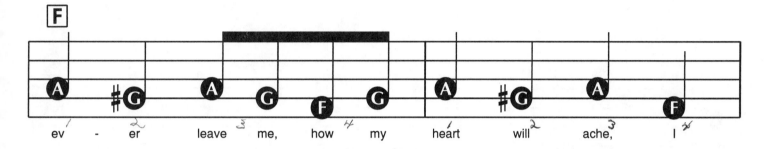

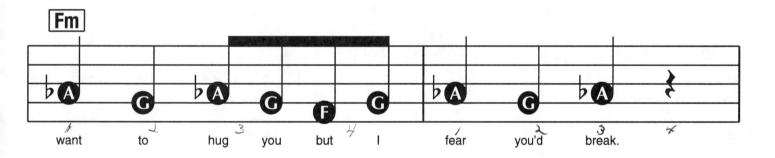

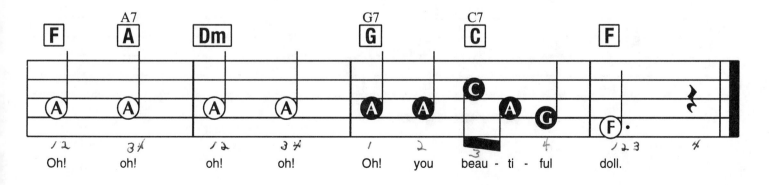

Over There

Registration 9
Rhythm: March

Words and Music by
George M. Cohan

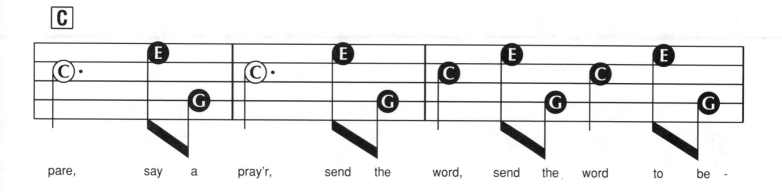

pare, say a pray'r, send the word, send the word to be -

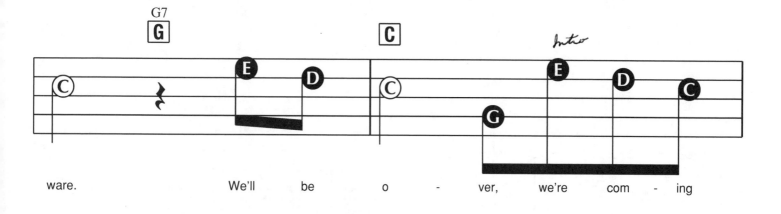

ware. We'll be o - ver, we're com - ing

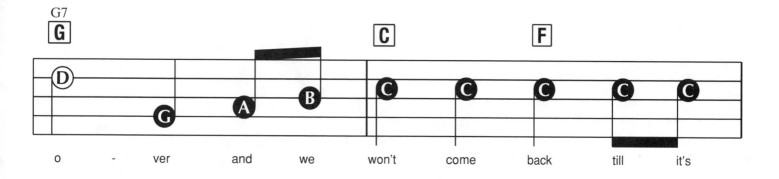

o - ver and we won't come back till it's

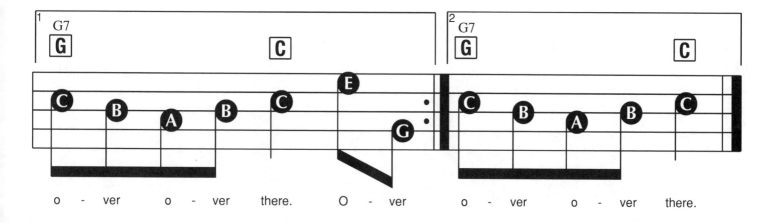

o - ver o - ver there. O - ver o - ver o - ver there.

Pack Up Your Troubles In Your Old Kit Bag And Smile, Smile, Smile

Registration 4
Rhythm: March

Words by George Asaf
Music by Felix Powell

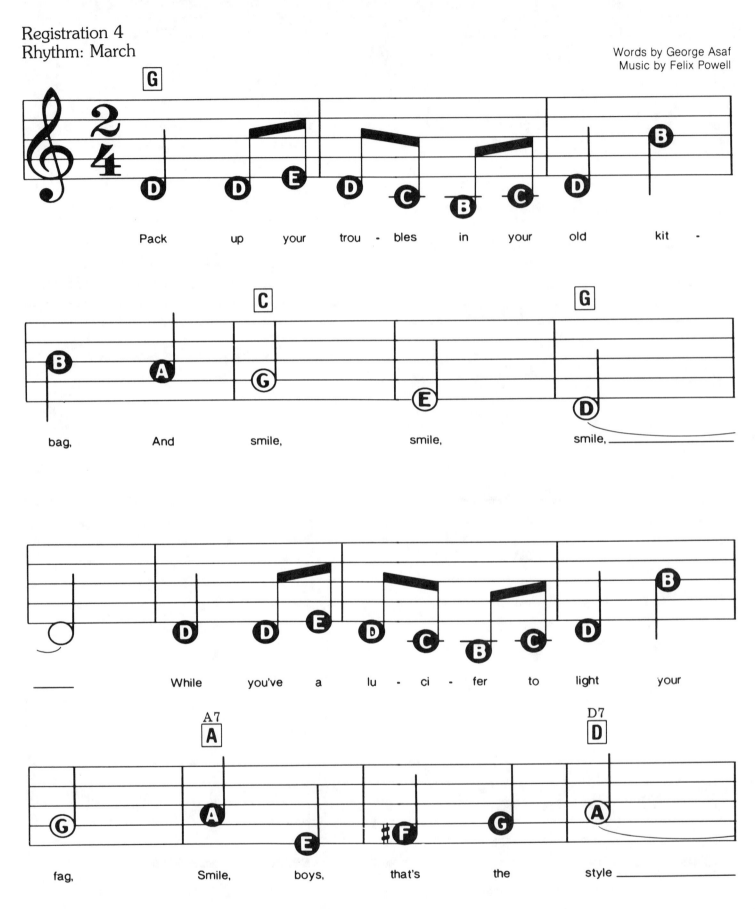

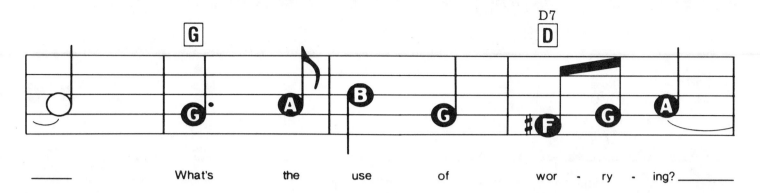

What's the use of wor - ry - ing? _____

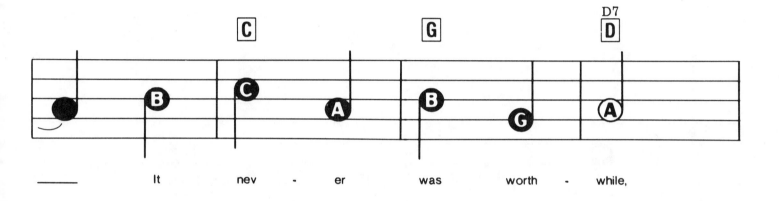

_____ It nev - er was worth - while,

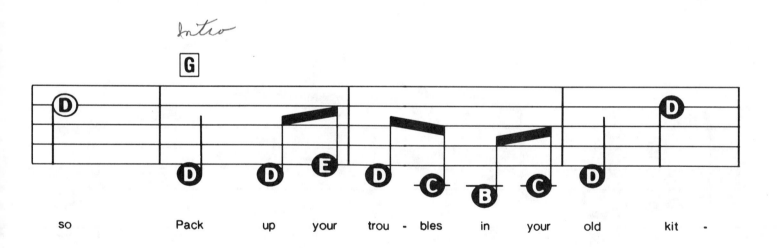

Intro

so Pack up your trou - bles in your old kit -

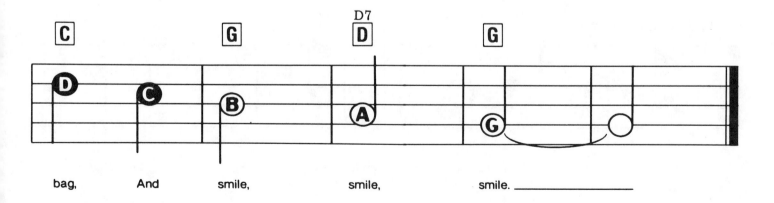

bag, And smile, smile, smile. _____

Peg O' My Heart

Registration 2
Rhythm: Fox Trot or Swing

Words by Alfred Bryan
Music by Fred Fisher

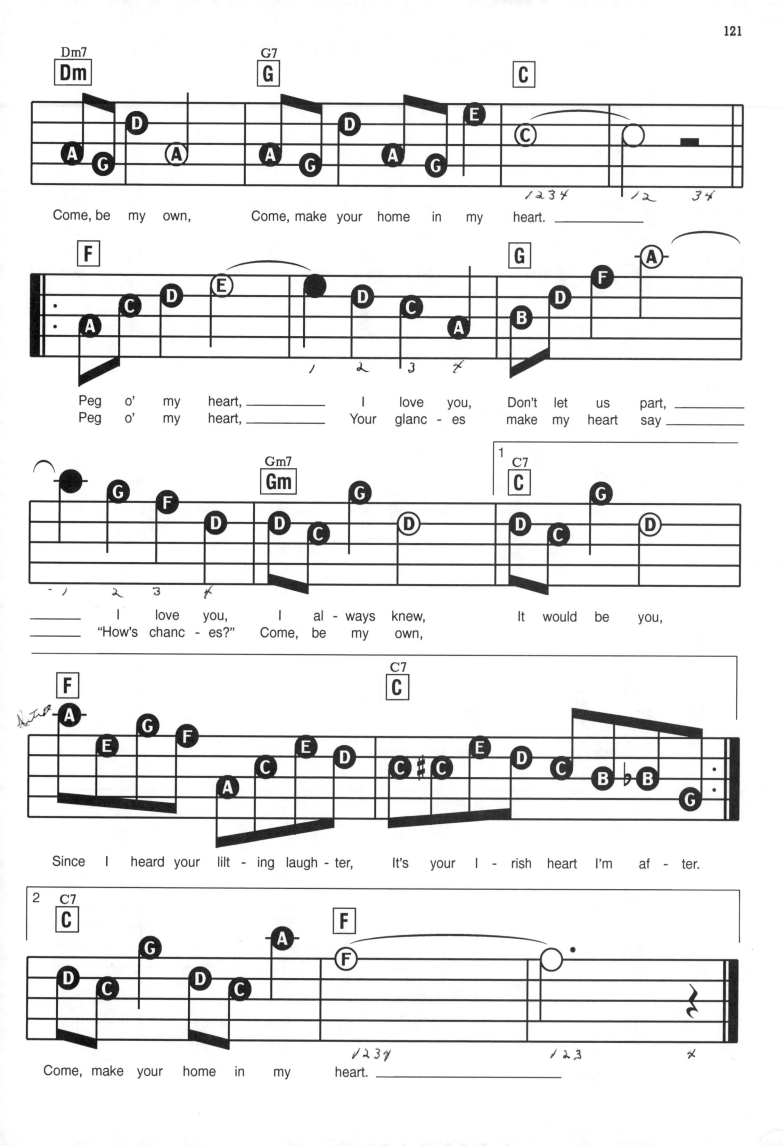

Play That Barbershop Chord

Registration 7
Rhythm: Fox-Trot

Words by William Tracey and Ballard MacDonald
Music by Lewis Muir

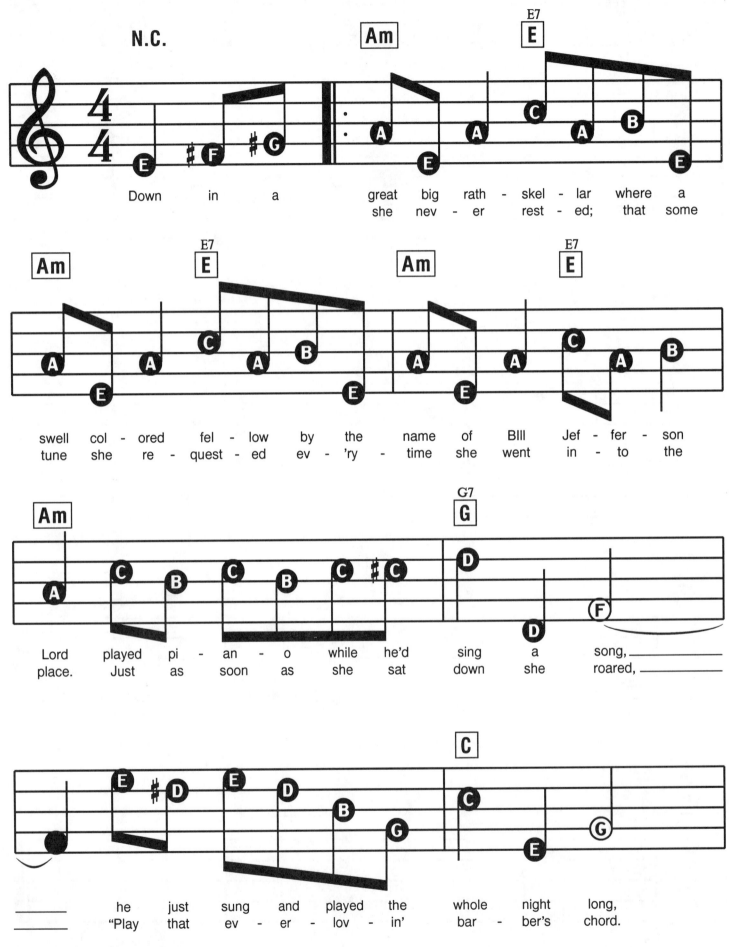

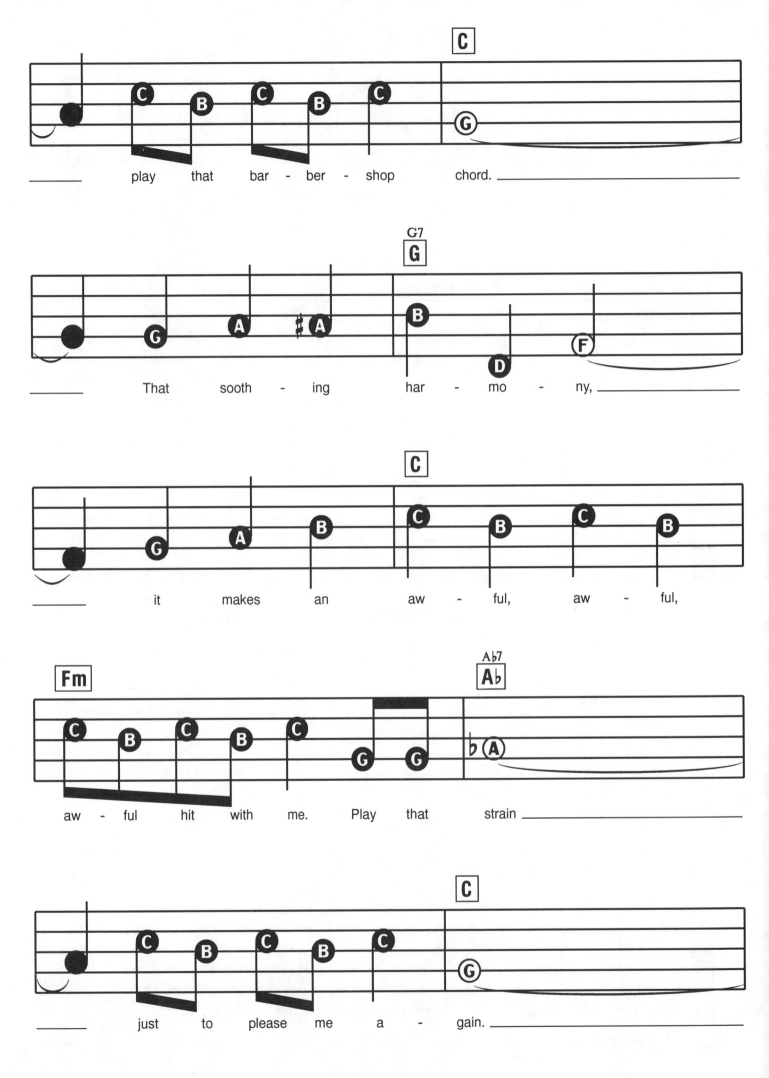

Put Your Arms Around Me, Honey

Registration 9
Rhythm: Fox Trot

Words by Junie McCree
Music by Albert Von Tilzer

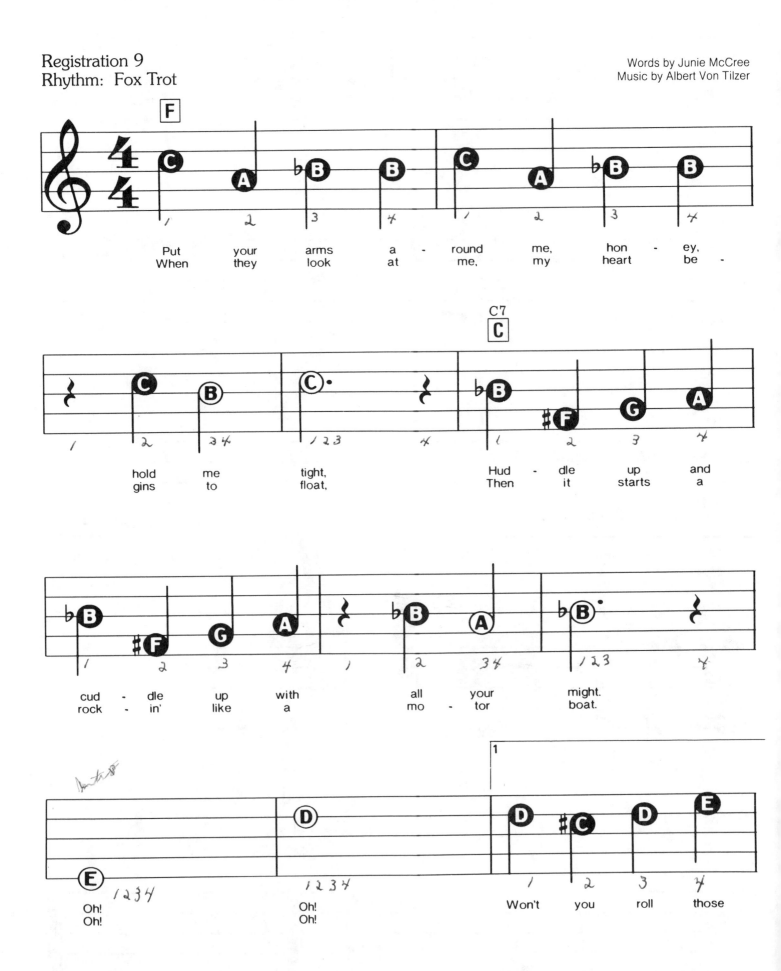

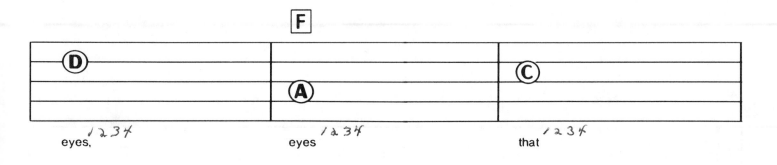

eyes, *1 2 3 4*   eyes *1 2 3 4*   that *1 2 3 4*

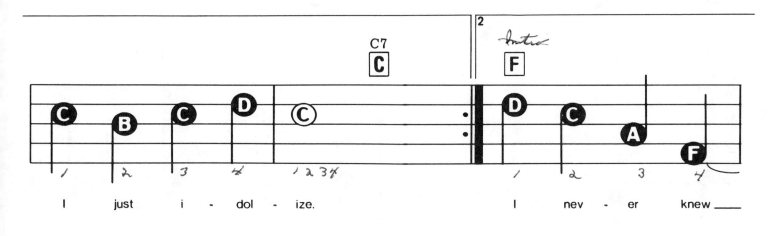

I just i - dol - ize.   I nev - er knew ____

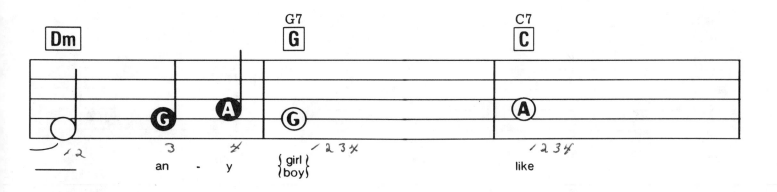

____ an - y {girl}{boy} like

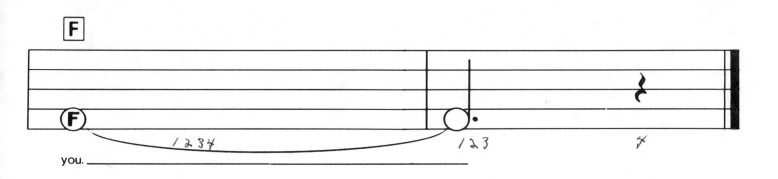

you. ____

The Sweetheart Of Sigma Chi

Words by Byron D. Stokes
Music by F. Dudleigh Vernor

Registration 1
Rhythm: Waltz

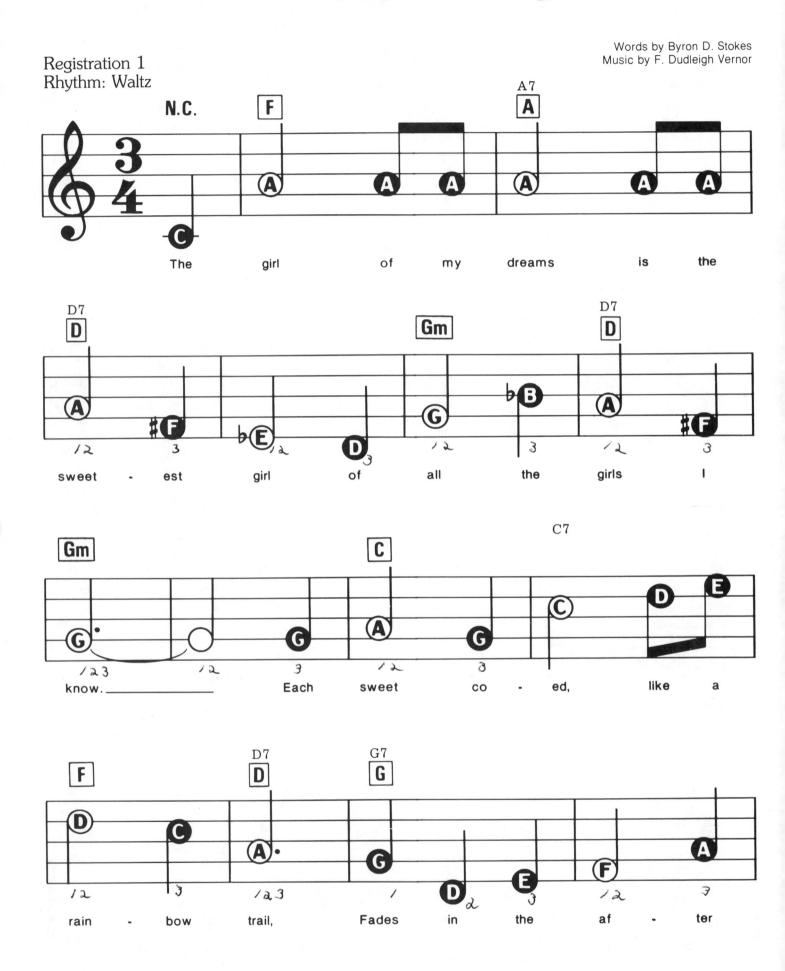

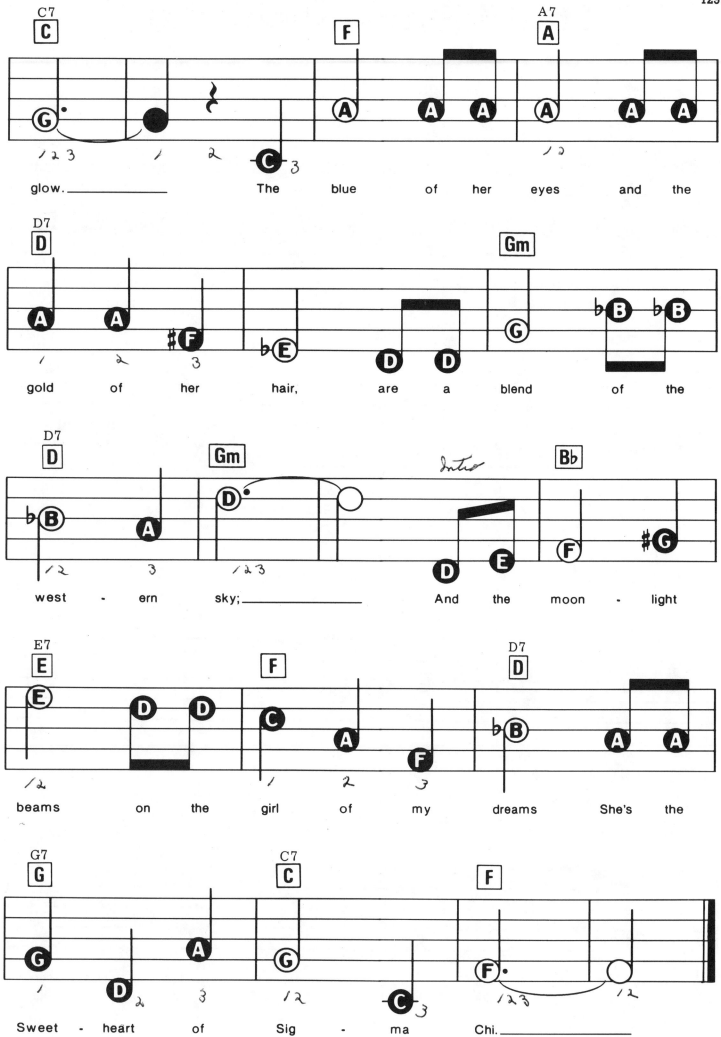

That International Rag

Registration 6
Rhythm: March

Words and Music by
Irving Berlin

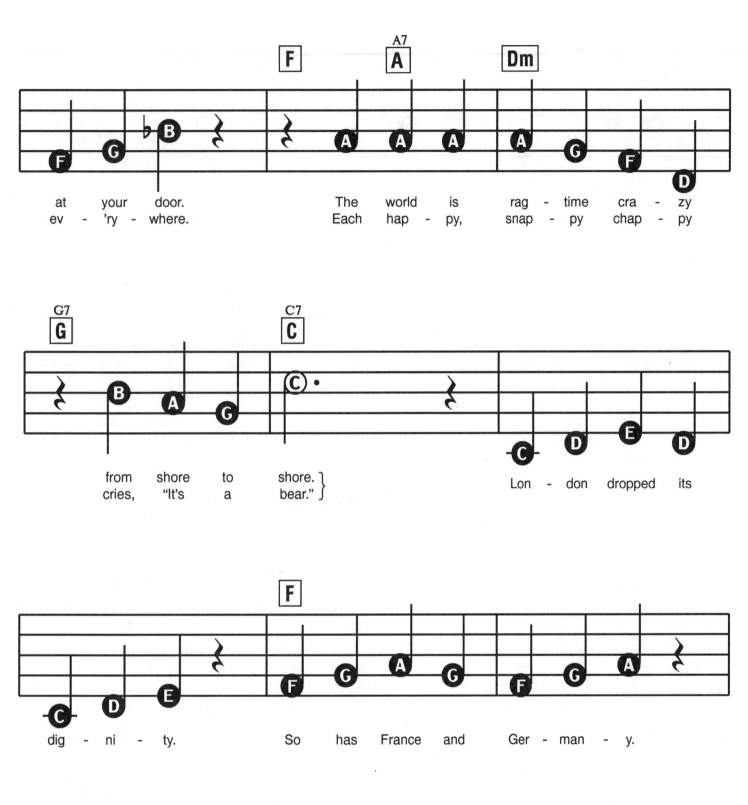

at your door. / ev - 'ry - where.   The world is rag - time cra - zy / Each hap - py, snap - py chap - py

from shore to shore. / cries, "It's a bear."   Lon - don dropped its

dig - ni - ty.   So has France and Ger - man - y.

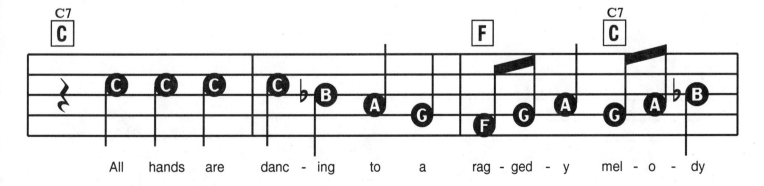

All hands are danc - ing to a rag - ged - y mel - o - dy

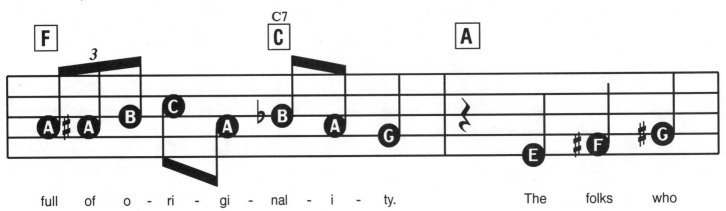

full of o - ri - gi - nal - i - ty. The folks who

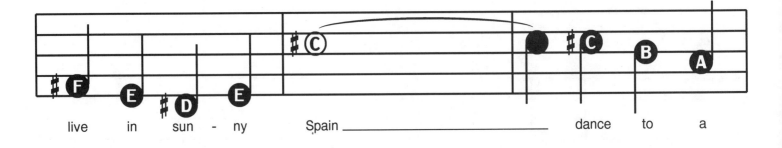

live in sun - ny Spain _____ dance to a

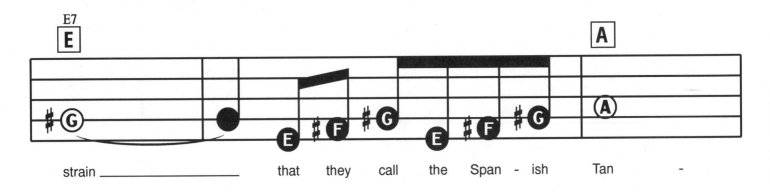

strain _____ that they call the Span - ish Tan -

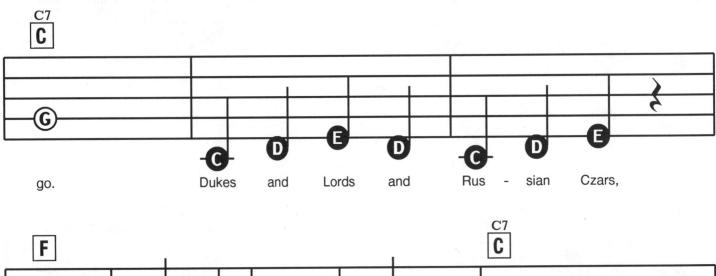

go. Dukes and Lords and Rus - sian Czars,

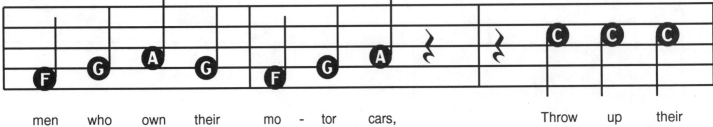

men who own their mo - tor cars, Throw up their

133

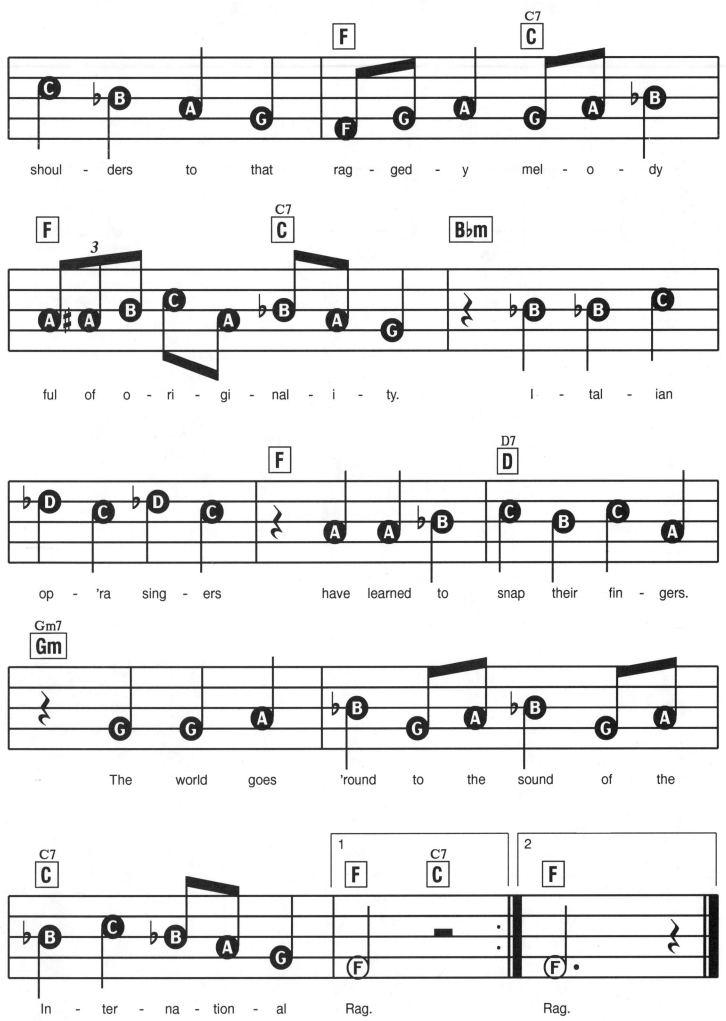

There's A Long, Long Trail

Registration 3
Rhythm: Fox Trot

Composed by Zo Elliot
Written by Stoddard King

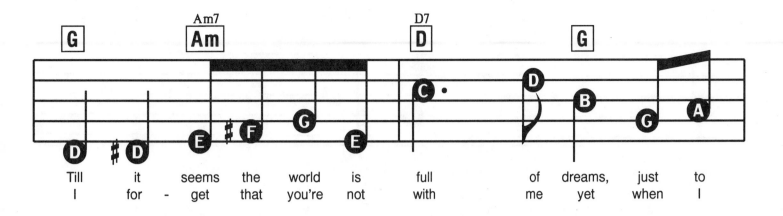

Till it seems the world is full of dreams, just to
I for - get that you're not with me yet when I

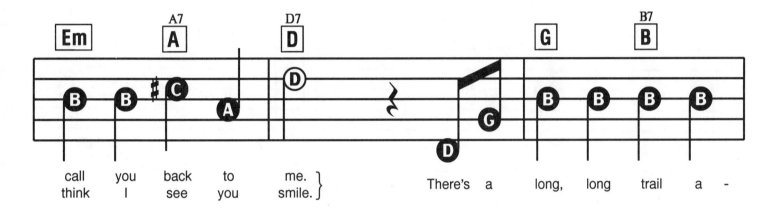

call you back to me. } There's a long, long trail a -
think I see you smile.

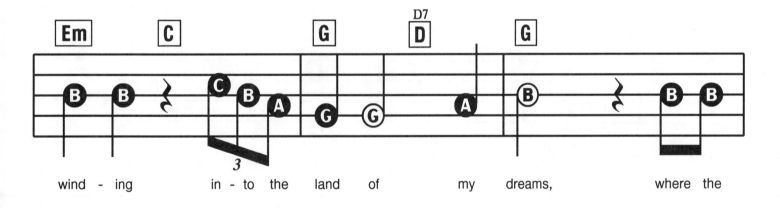

wind - ing in - to the land of my dreams, where the

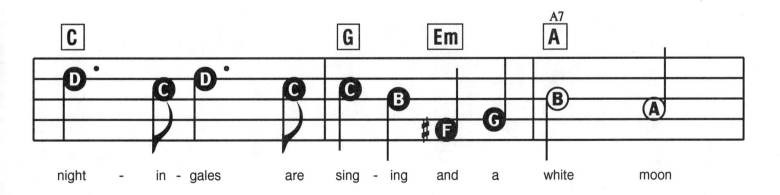

night - in - gales are sing - ing and a white moon

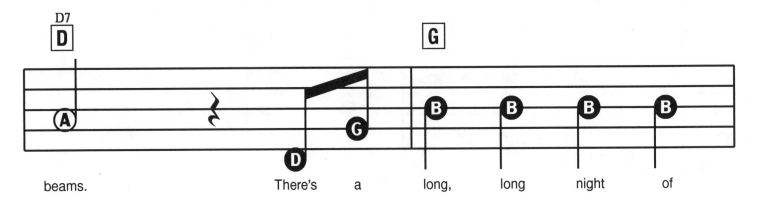

beams. There's a long, long night of

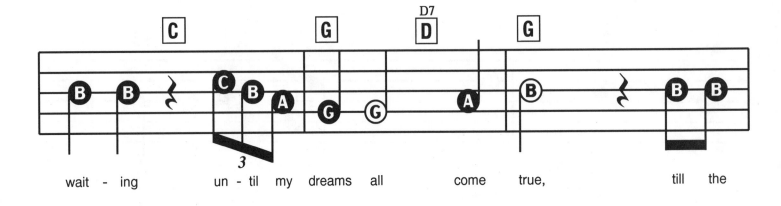

wait - ing un - til my dreams all come true, till the

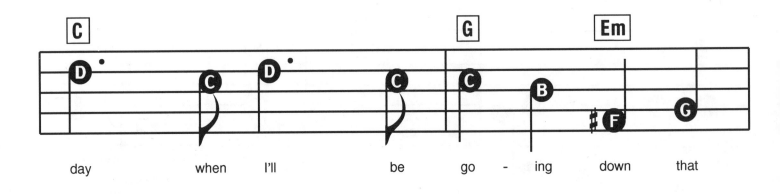

day when I'll be go - ing down that

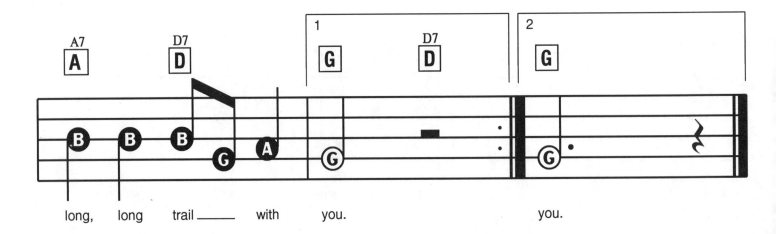

long, long trail _____ with you. you.

The Trail Of The Lonesome Pine

Registration 7
Rhythm: Fox Trot

Words by Ballard MacDonald
Music by Harry Carroll

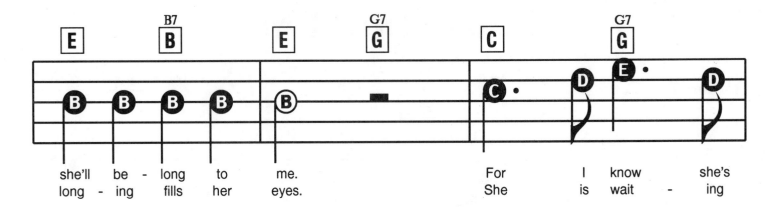

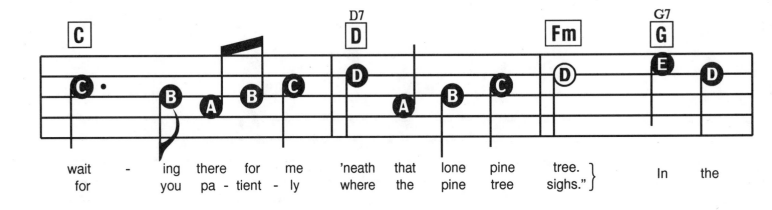

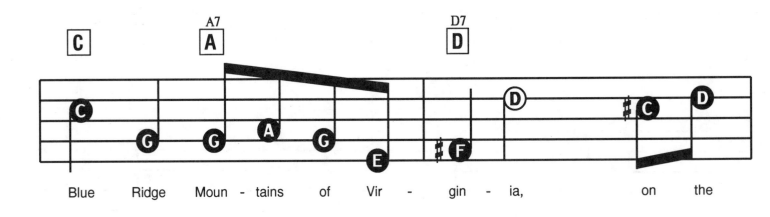

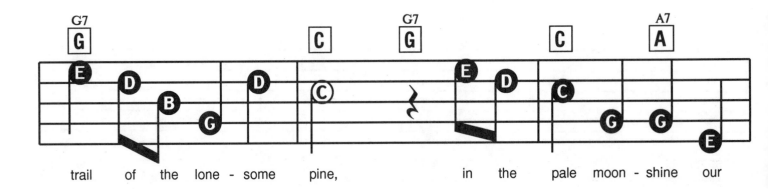

They Didn't Believe Me

Registration 2
Rhythm: Ballad or Swing

Words by Herbert Reynolds
Music by Jerome Kern

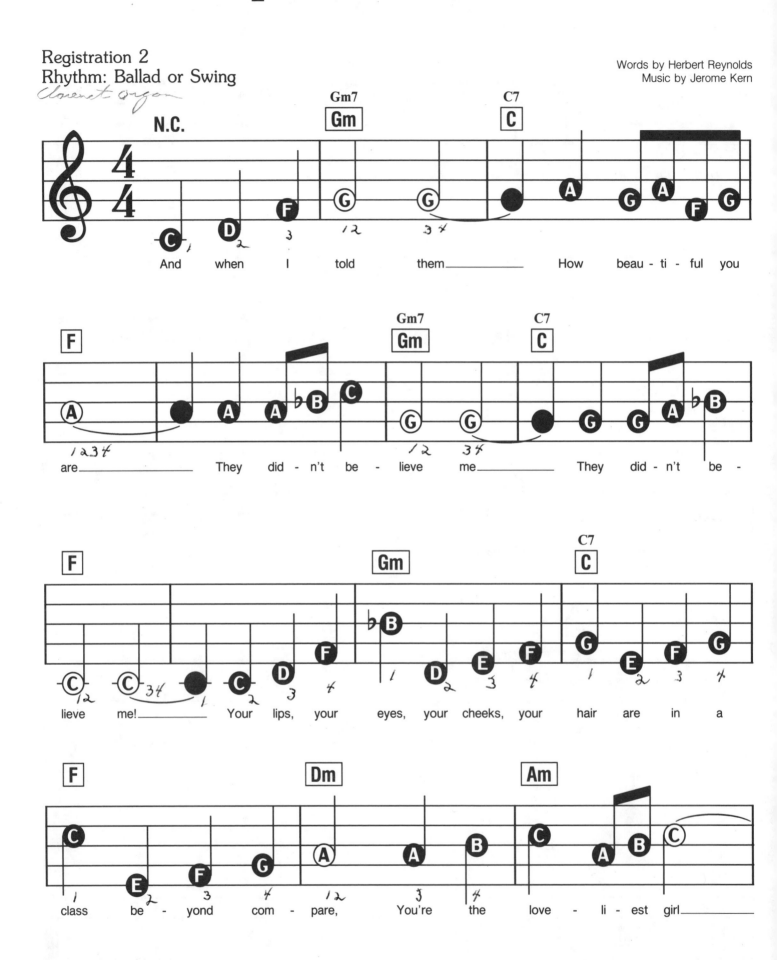

141

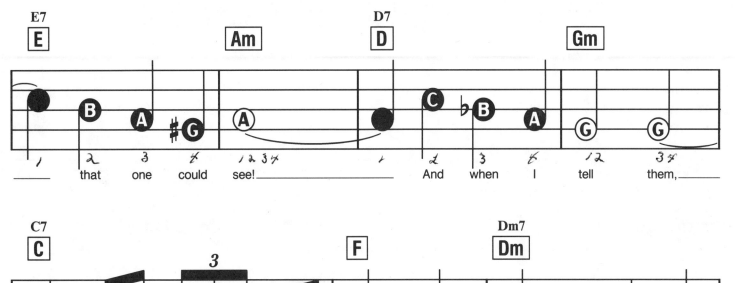

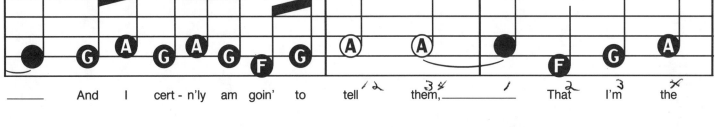

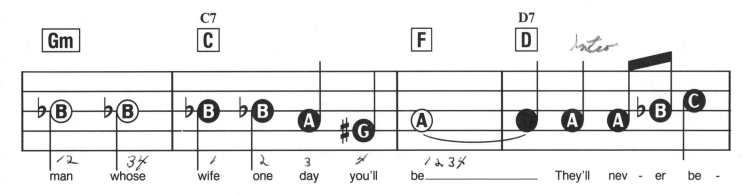

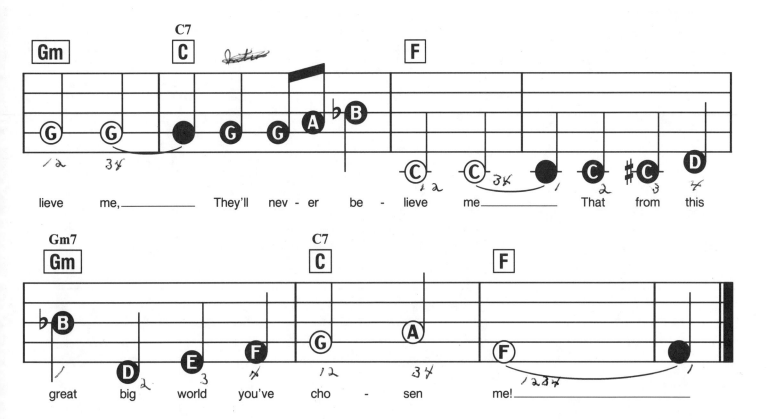

Till The Clouds Roll By

Registration 1
Rhythm: Fox Trot or Swing

Words and Music by Jerome Kern
and P.G. Wodehouse

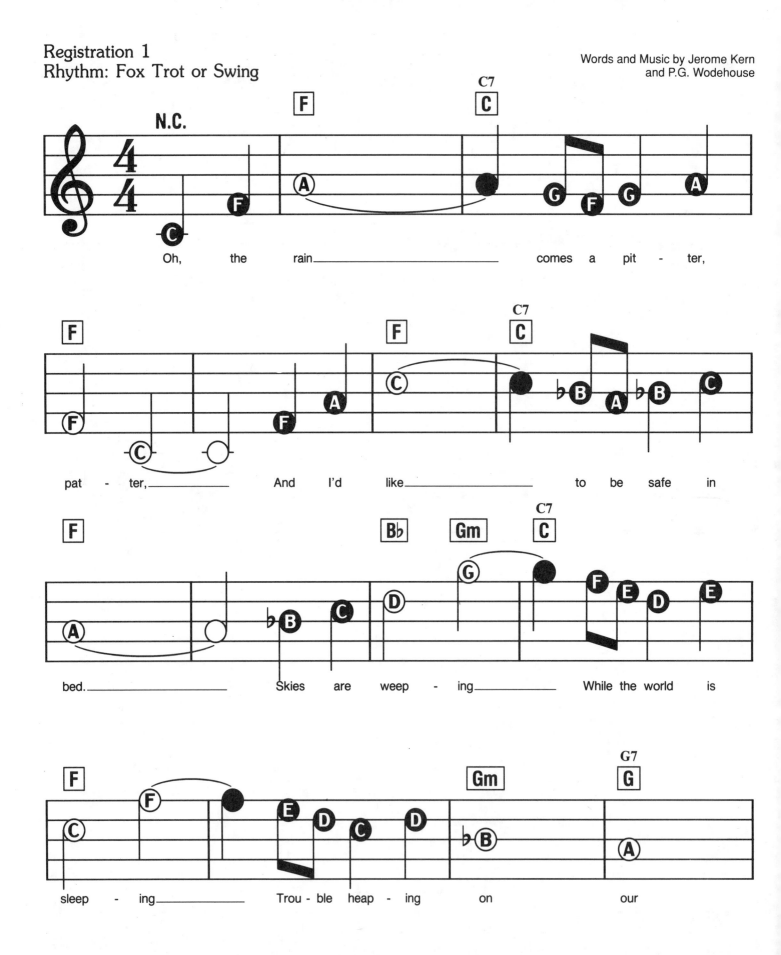

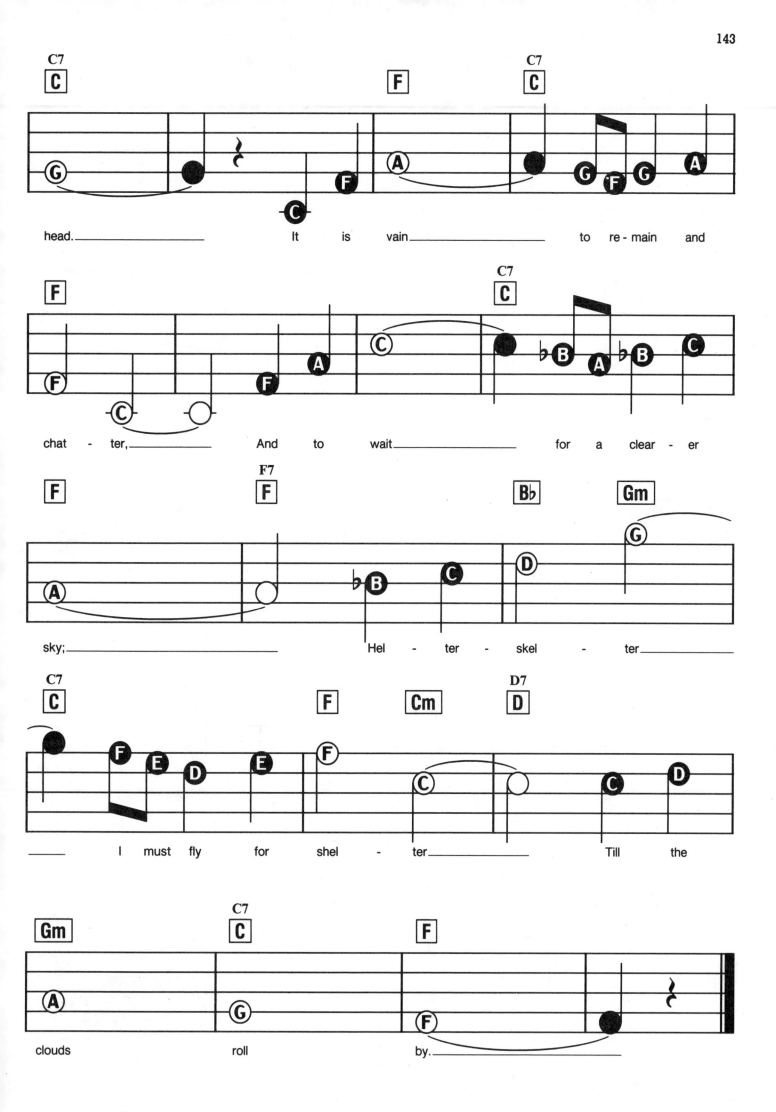

To The Land Of My Own Romance

Registration 3
Rhythm: Waltz

Music by Victor Herbert
Lyric by Harry B. Smith

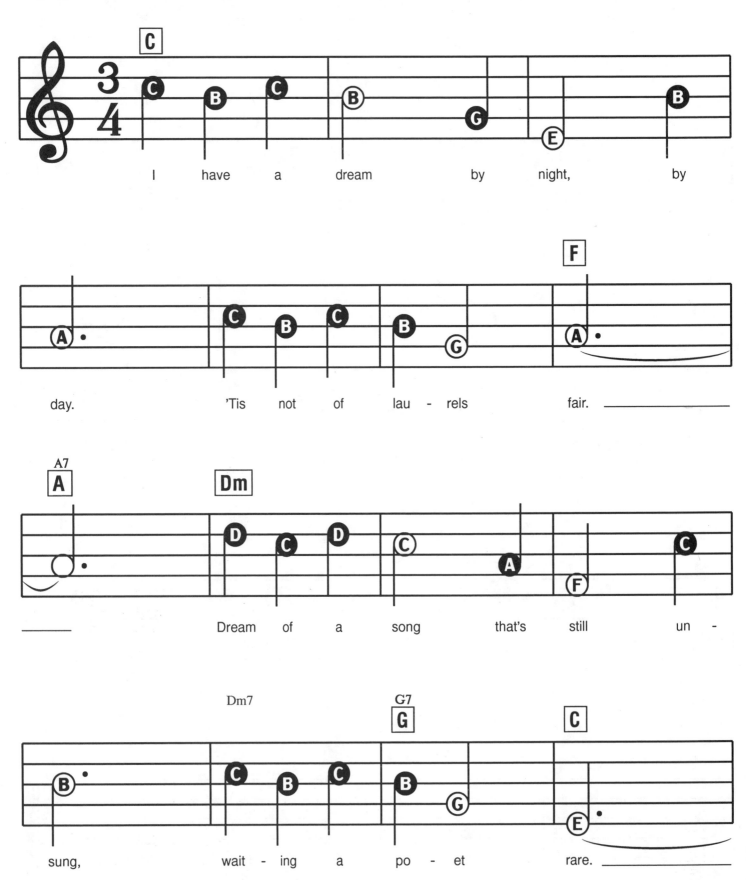

I have a dream by night, by

day. 'Tis not of lau - rels fair. _____

_____ Dream of a song that's still un -

sung, wait - ing a po - et rare. _____

145

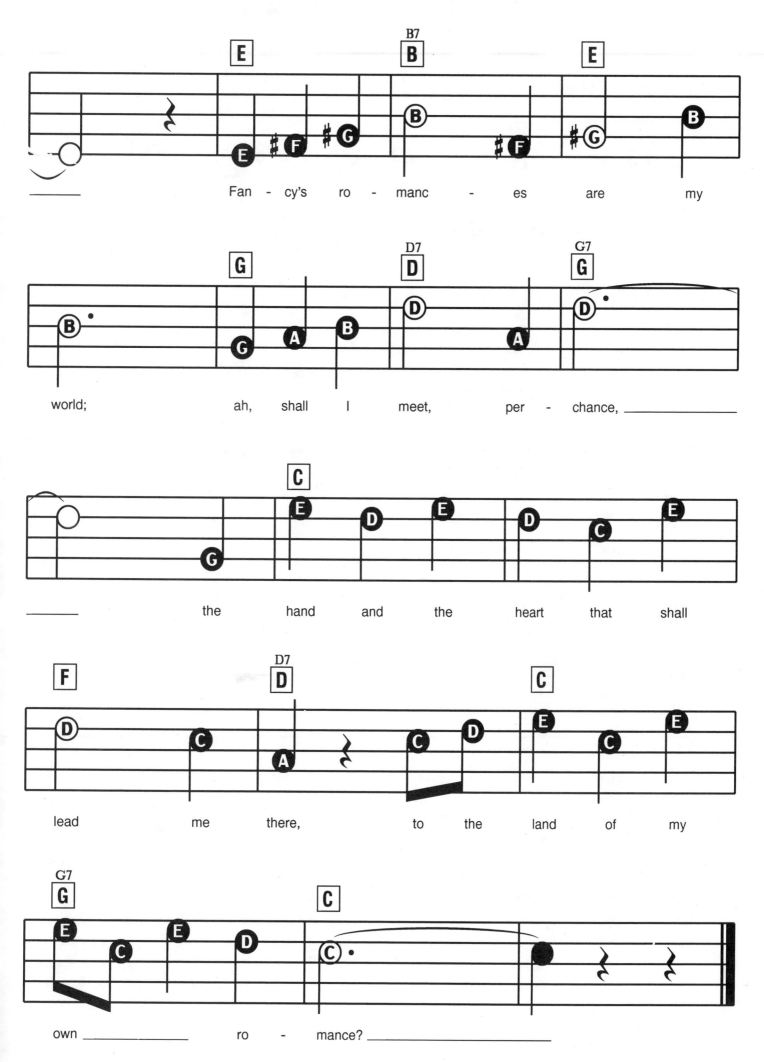

12th Street Rag

Registration 5
Rhythm: Shuffle or Swing

By Euday L. Bowman

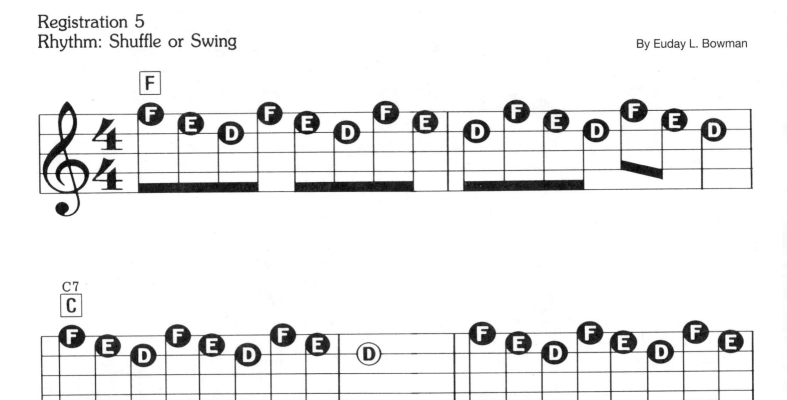

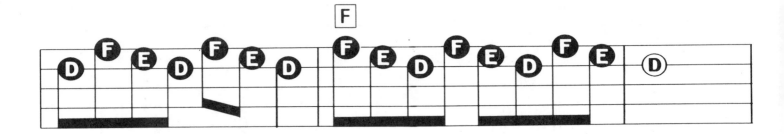

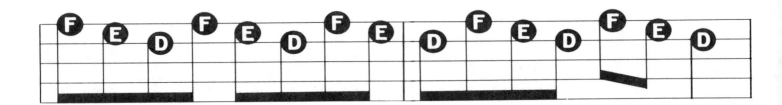

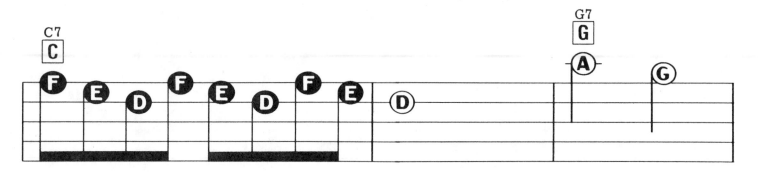

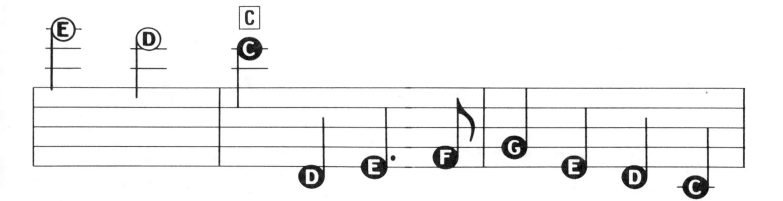

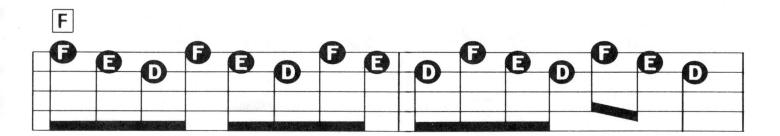

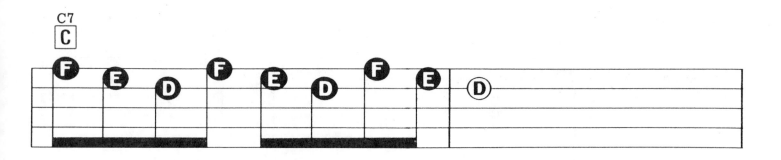

148

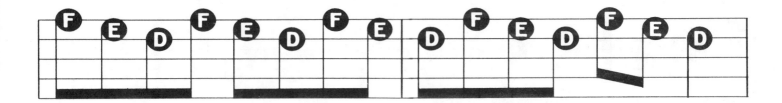

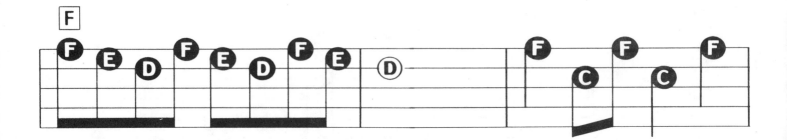

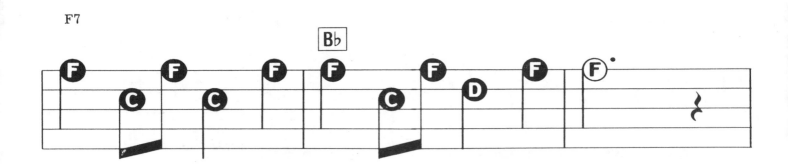

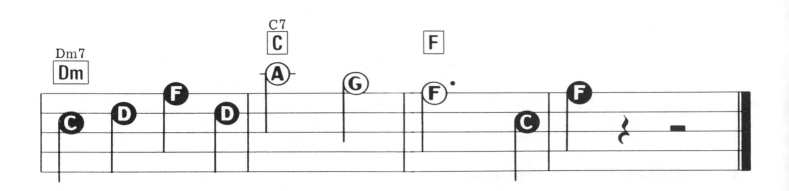

Wee Wee Marie

Registration 7
Rhythm: March

Music by Fred Fisher
Words by Alfred Bryan and Joe McCarthy

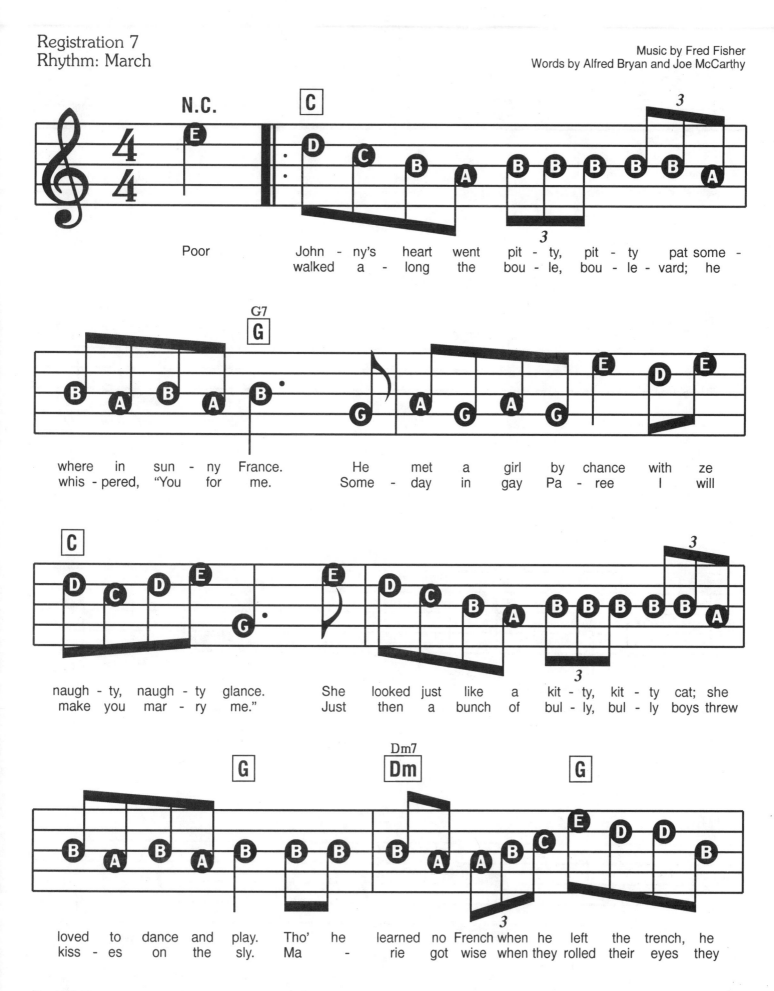

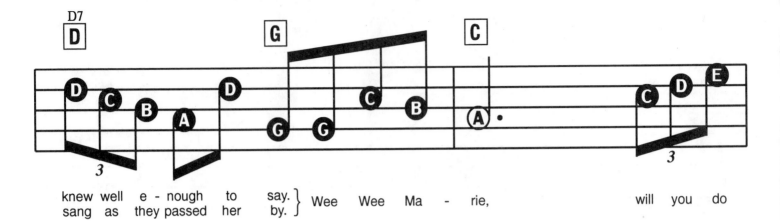

knew well e - nough to say. } Wee Wee Ma - rie, will you do
sang as they passed her by. }

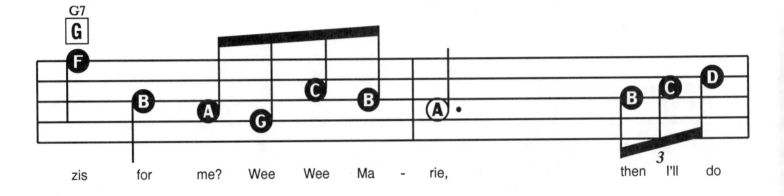

zis for me? Wee Wee Ma - rie, then I'll do

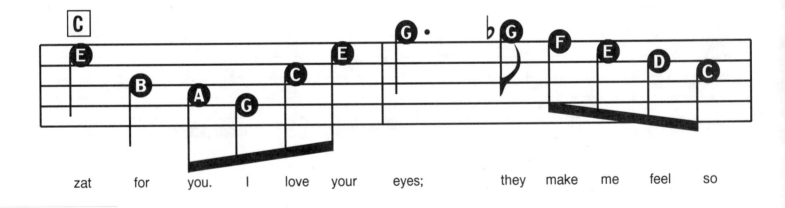

zat for you. I love your eyes; they make me feel so

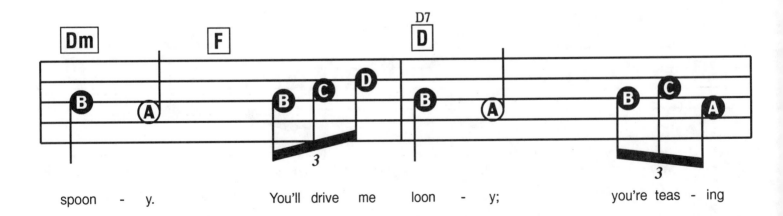

spoon - y. You'll drive me loon - y; you're teas - ing

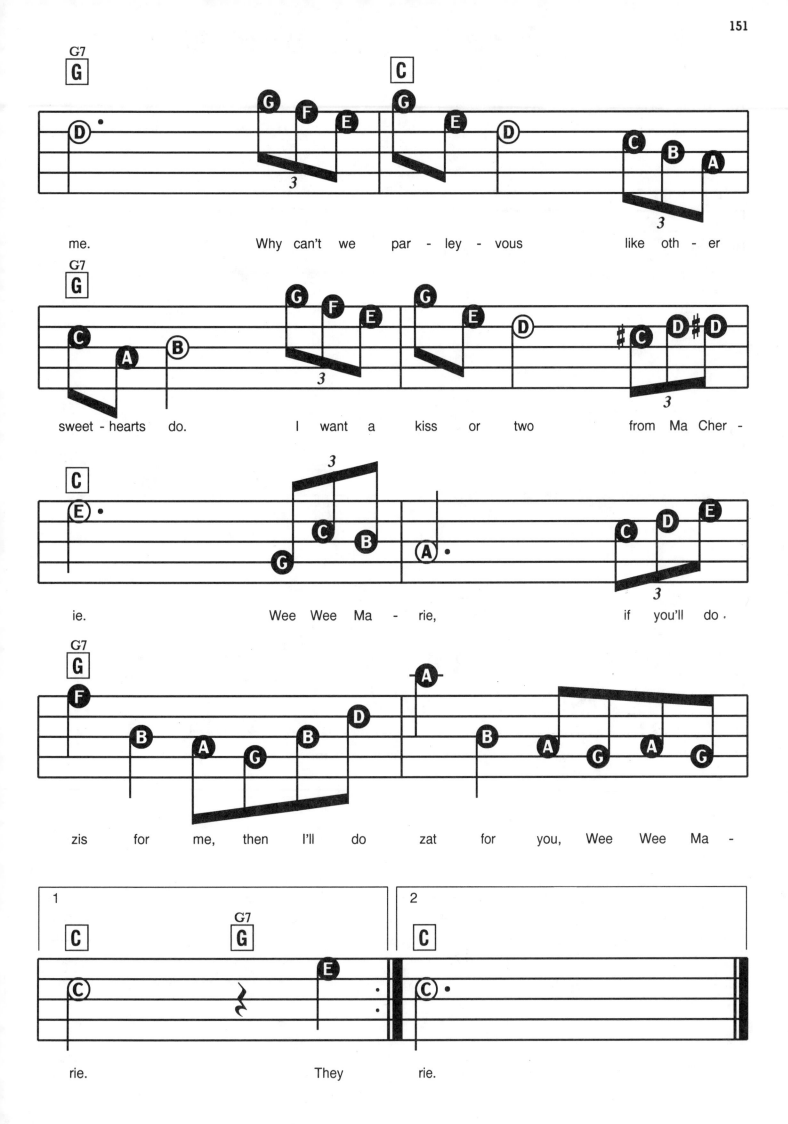

Waiting For The Robert E. Lee

Registration 3
Rhythm: Fox Trot or Jazz

Words by L. Wolfe Gilbert
Music by Lewis F. Muir

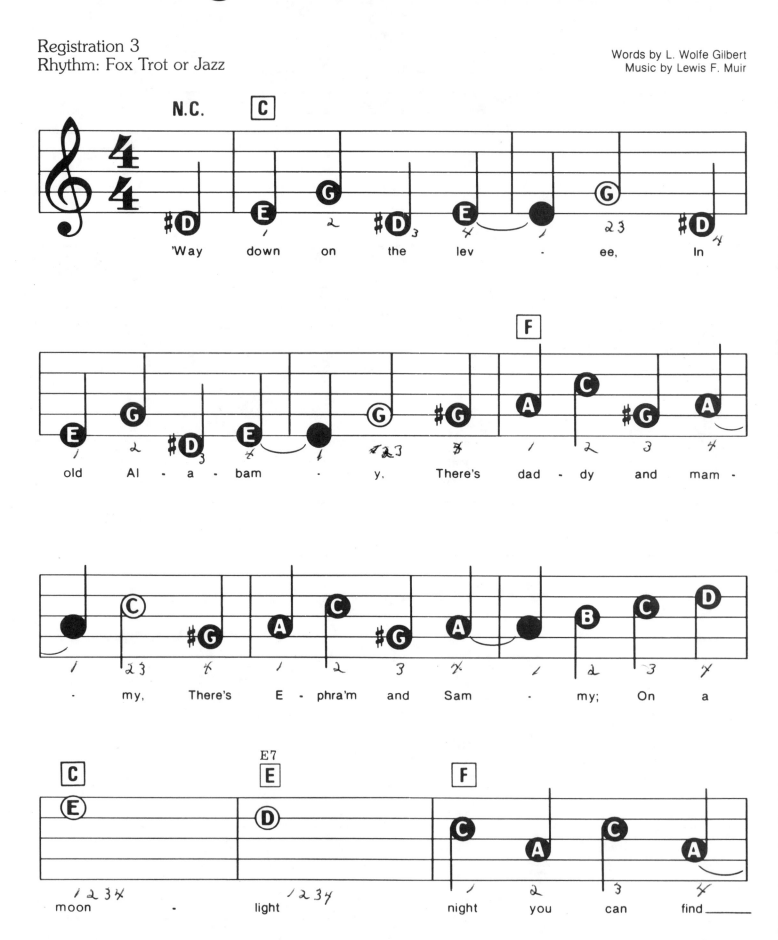

153

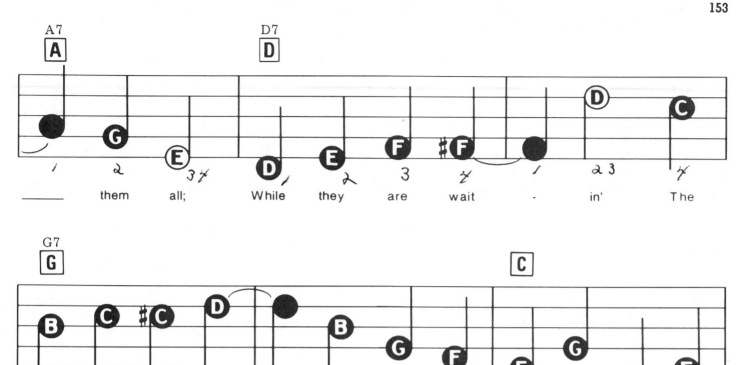

them ____ all; While they are wait - in' The

ban - jos are syn - co - pat - in'; What's that they're say -

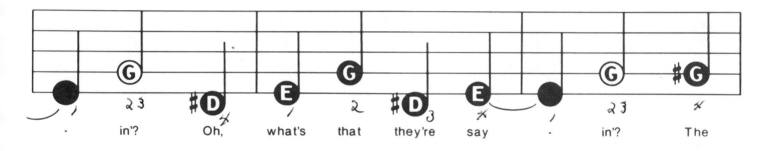

- in'? Oh, what's that they're say - in'? The

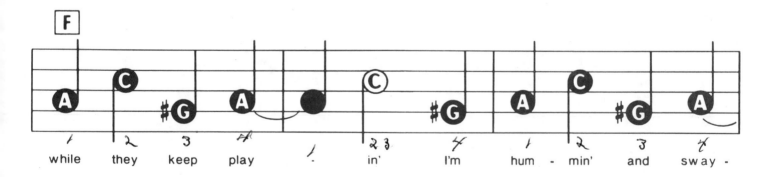

while they keep play - in' I'm hum - min' and sway -

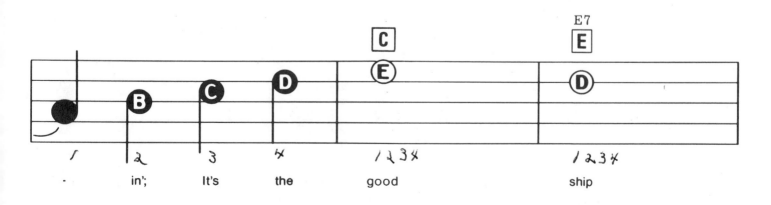

- in'; It's the good ship

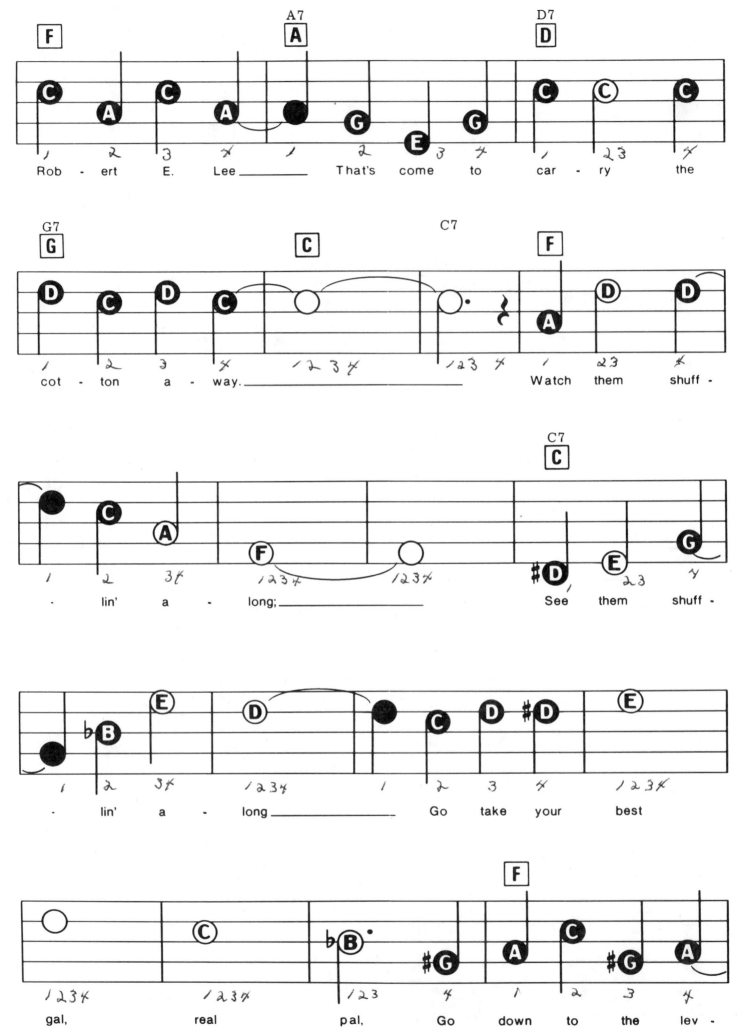

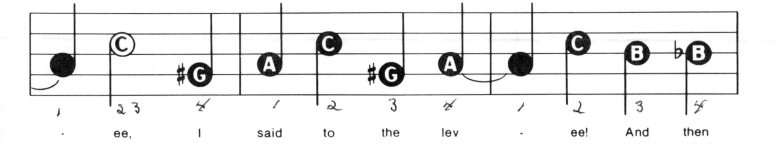

- ee, I said to the lev - ee! And then

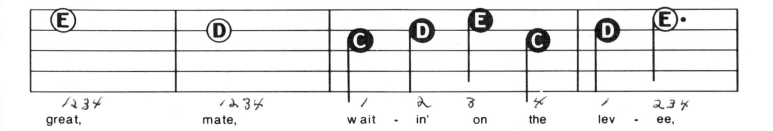

join that shuff - - lin' throng;_____

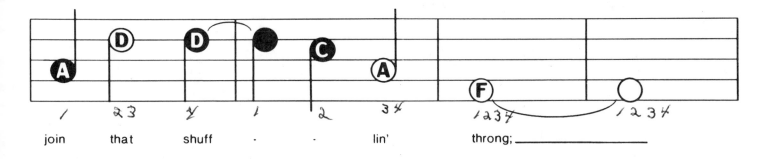

Hear that mu - sic and song;_____ It's sim - ply

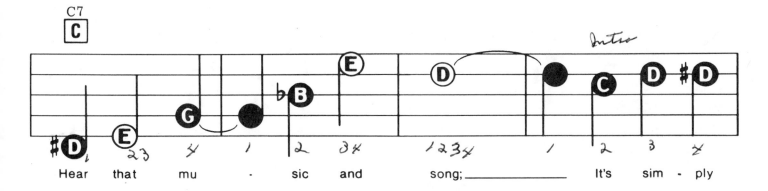

great, mate, wait - in' on the lev - ee,

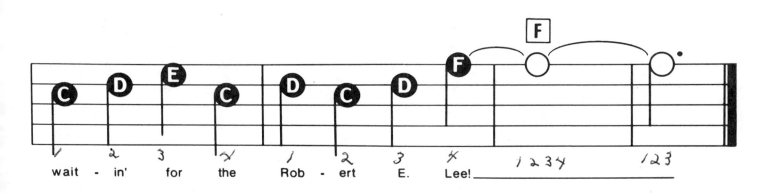

wait - in' for the Rob - ert E. Lee!_____

When Irish Eyes Are Smiling

Registration 3
Rhythm: Waltz

Words by Chauncey Olcott and George Graff Jr.
Music by Ernest R. Ball

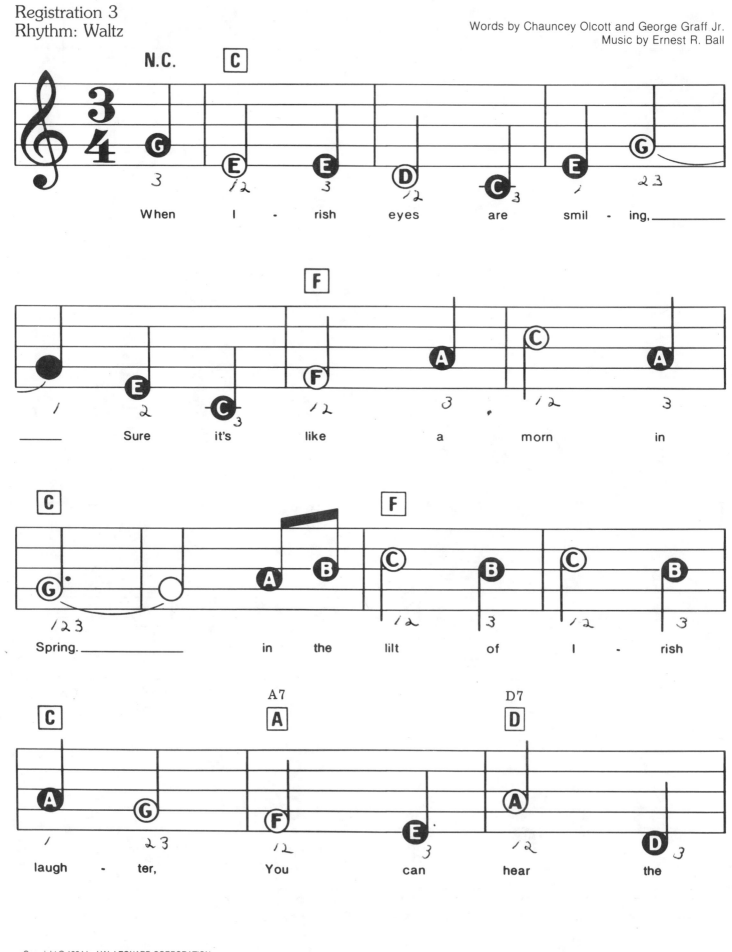

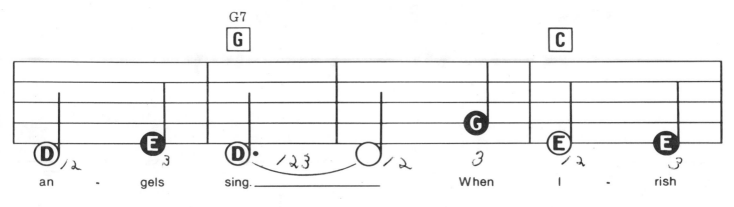

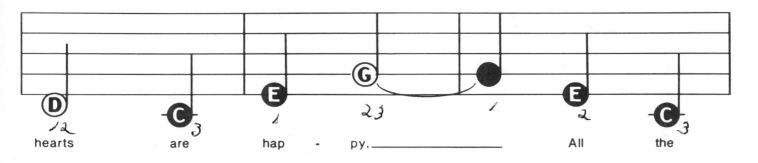

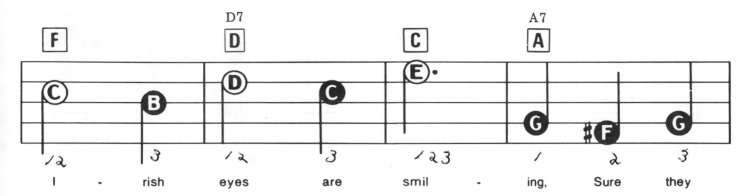

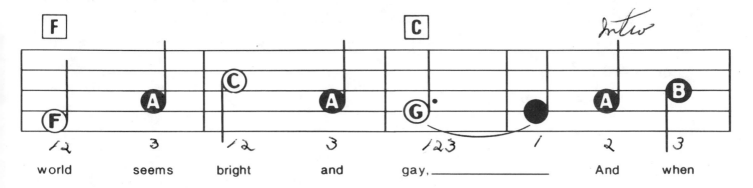

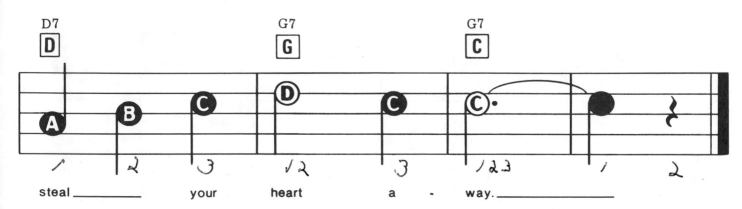

When It's Apple Blossom Time In Normandy

Registration 1
Rhythm: Fox Trot

Written and Composed by
Mellor Gifford and Trevor

On a farm in Nor - man - dy,
Said Ma - rie, "It's clear to me,
Ap - ple blos - som time soon came;

there re - sid - ed Rose Ma - rie.
tho' sin - cere you seem to be,
Rose Ma - rie then changed her name.

She was the pride of the coun - try - side,
I am a - fraid of the prom - ise made; you
For with the spring he had brought the ring

fair as a maid could be.
may not come back to me.
his lov - ing bride to claim.

Came a lov - er, bold one
By the wish - ing well to -
By the wish - ing well they

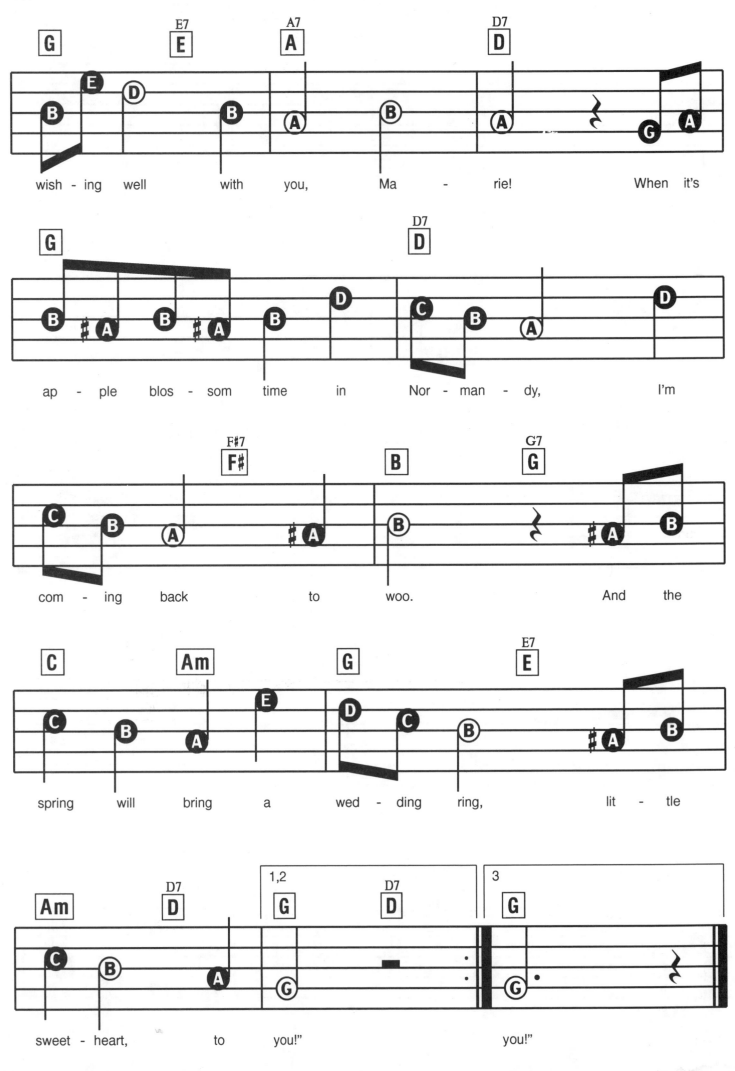

You Made Me Love You
(I Didn't Want To Do It)

Registration 7
Rhythm: Fox Trot

Words by Joe McCarthy
Music by James V. Monaco

162

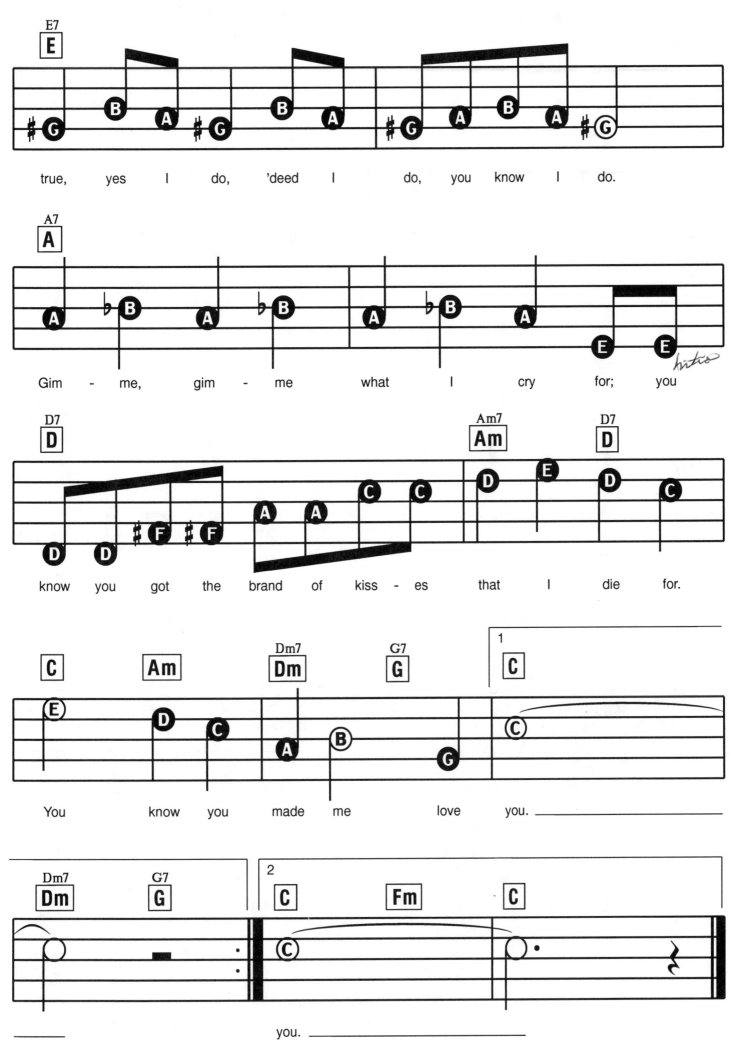

You Can't Stop The Yanks

Registration 4
Rhythm: March

Words and Music by
Jack Caddigan and Chick Story

Ev - 'ry - where A - mer - i - can hearts are
Ev - 'ry - where A - mer - i - ca's sons are

feel - ing gay, just be - cause A -
go - ing strong. They are on - ly

mer - i - ca's start - ed on her way.
help - ing the French to right a wrong.

Yan - kees long and thin, hik - ing to Ber -
Hav - ing lots of fun pick - ing off the

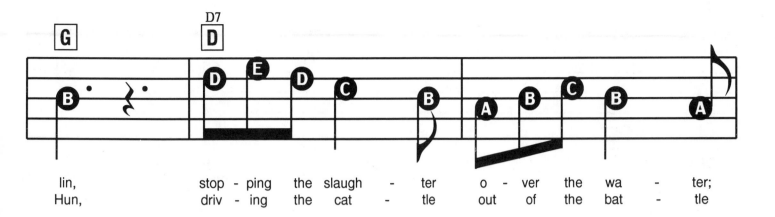

lin,   stop - ping the slaugh - ter   o - ver the wa - ter;
Hun,   driv - ing the cat - tle   out of the bat - tle

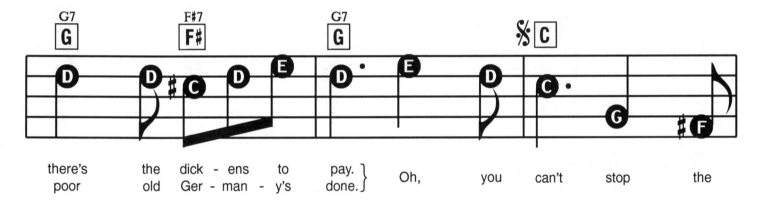

there's   the dick - ens to pay.   Oh,   you can't stop the
poor   old Ger - man - y's done.

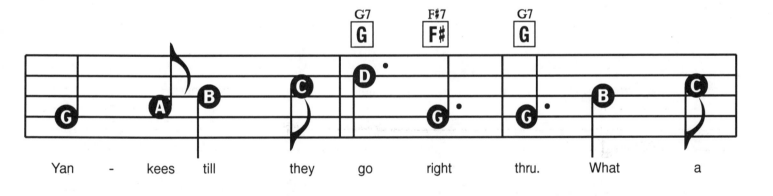

Yan - kees till   they go right thru. What a

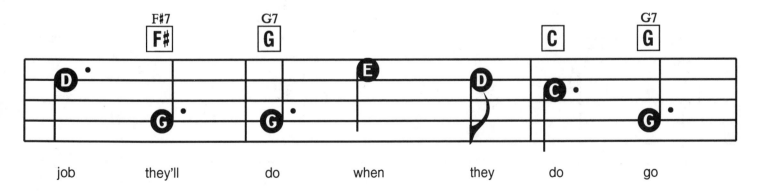

job they'll   do when   they do go

166

Registration Guide

- Match the Registration number on the song to the corresponding numbered category below. Select and activate an instrumental sound available on your instrument.

- Choose an automatic rhythm appropriate to the mood and style of the song. (Consult your Owner's Guide for proper operation of automatic rhythm features.)

- Adjust the tempo and volume controls to comfortable settings.

Registration

1	Flute, Pan Flute, Jazz Flute
2	Clarinet, Organ
3	Violin, Strings
4	Brass, Trumpet, Bass
5	Synth Ensemble, Accordion, Brass
6	Pipe Organ, Harpsichord
7	Jazz Organ, Vibraphone, Vibes, Electric Piano, Jazz Guitar
8	Piano, Electric Piano
9	Trumpet, Trombone, Clarinet, Saxophone, Oboe
10	Violin, Cello, Strings